Charting Success

Walking Away from the Lie to Find Your Success

Billy Thompson

"Rather than following what *others* define as success,
I help people find THEIR success."

Cataloged in publication information is available from Library and Archives U.S.

ISBN:978-1-956257-49-6

Publishing by Pierucci Publishing

Cover design by Pierucci Publishing, Billy Thompson and Julie Husch

Contributors: Jonathan Grant, Dale and Hannah Chaplin, and Jill Thompson

Interior design by Sophie Hanks, and Jill and Billy Thompson

To Anyone Looking for Success

I wrote this book to support and help people. I wrote this book because I know everyone can navigate toward the best version of themselves and that we can all find *our* version of success. If you or anyone you know would benefit from a conversation to discover their path, I am available.

You can reach me at: chartingsuccess@lumegent.com

COURSE SETTING

If you Google my name, Billy Thompson, you'll see that I'm not a former Scottish soccer player nor an ex-NBA player. You don't know me. Not yet.

There are millions of business books and even more memoirs and autobiographies. This book is neither, yet both. This book isn't your average read defined into a single category.

I wrote this book the same way I teach, using my life experiences to provide lessons. I've faced many unique situations in my life. I hope to be raw about it all; I hope to show some vulnerability in the chapters that form this book. I hope you get a feel for the type of human being I am. Because that's how *connections* are made—and *connection* is what I am about.

Why should you want to listen to me?

I started from less than nothing in my life, with countless obstacles. I've faced abuse, abandonment, and death, among other adversities. I wasn't born with opportunities; I had to create them. The world was against me. But I overcame it.

I've now built several multi-million-dollar companies, worked with Fortune 500 companies, and created success for numerous clients, personally and professionally. I've consulted, coached, and mentored in all walks of life. I've spent my entire life behind the scenes, putting my success before my ego, and thus you've never heard of me. Until today.

I may not appear on Google, but I work when I want, and don't work when I choose. I have financial freedom; I have the house my wife wanted and take the vacations my family deserves. I can decide where my time goes. I never miss my daughter's volleyball games; I have dates with my wife and time with my friends and family. I control my time and my life. But most of all, I get to define what my life is, not what the world tells me it should be.

So, once again, *why should you want to listen to me?*

Because, through adversity, I discovered what success is and the formula for each person to find theirs.

This book is not a typical business book. It isn't a "5-Steps to a…" type book. It isn't a late-night infomercial stating that you are guaranteed to make millions by Tuesday by purchasing the program! It is not that book; I do not provide some fortune cookie advice. I feel that most people will never find success by following steps. If that were true, we'd have ninety-eight percent of the population as millionaires, all from buying a single book.

Before someone can follow steps, they first need to change their mentality. The approach I take in this book is to shift your attitude, change your mentality, and teach through my experiences. Most people I meet start from step negative three. In this mindset, they'll never reach step one, let alone be able to pursue further success.

Additionally, the world is going to tell you that you are bound to the life you were born into, as I call it your "Generational Cycle". This is a *lie*, this is how the game is rigged.

We are expected to follow the life we are given, expected to follow what the world tells you is SUCCESS. You don't have to play this rigged game, there is another way. This book is here to help.

As you read, take the time to see the lesson in each chapter, how it applies to life, and how it applies to business, but mostly how it applies to finding success.

What I discuss is genuine, so I use my personal experiences to teach. This book is a series of experiences I've faced, which gives the vibe of a memoir/autobiography. But if you take the time to *see* it, you will discover that there is a lesson with each experience I share. This approach is unusual to the practice of a business book, but it is precisely how attitudes and mentalities are changed. I am a consultant, coach, and mentor. My mission is to help people find *their* version of success. This approach can transform thoughts into clarity and dreams into reality.

As you read through the experiences in my life, at the minimum, you'll be entertained, but mostly I hope you can realize the direction for your own life. I am often asked about my decision to make the drastic changes I made. The course I took, switching away from what I thought was success to find MY SUCCESS, was anything but traditional. What I walked away from is unbelievable to most, you'll soon see, but I always have the same response: "Best decision of my life. I've never been more successful."

As you join my journey, each chapter will ultimately add up to the realization I have reached, and hopefully, you'll learn something about yourself along the way.

CONTENTS

FOREWORD

By

Ren Thompson

(Billy's Daughter)

I guess the best way to begin would be with a quote. You'll quickly learn how fitting it is: "It's not easy growing up in a house where someone knows your every thought or thinks they do." It's from the TV show Lie To Me, but the moment I heard it, I knew I felt the same.

I grew up in a home where my father, whom I call PaPâ, seemed to understand my every thought and emotion. His unique life has created superpower-like abilities that could be made into a TV show. But this isn't fiction. This is the true story of my father.

My father and I are very similar. I love him, but this can be challenging. We have an excellent relationship. I was able to grow up in a stable environment. He was not.

Our life runs in parallels. His father was gone a lot when he was little, and so was mine. His father was lost to drugs, alcohol, and other issues, but mine was gone for better reasons. His father wanted a better life for him; mine does as well.

You'll soon read that to achieve a better life for himself and for me, my PaPâ worked hard. Too hard. He pushed himself to unbelievable lengths to provide me with the life I am in, and for that, I'll love and appreciate him forever.

To describe this book is challenging. I first said, "It's different reading about it than growing up with the stories he told around me. This is the raw truth." It's overwhelming to hear, almost unbelievable. I wonder how my friends' parents will react, to be honest.

I'm only 14, and I already know that few people have experienced what he has. There is much sadness, betrayal, and heartbreak. As you read, you may feel sadness or pity for what he faced, but my PaPâ would say, "Nonsense, look at what it gave me."

It's fascinating to hear how my dad went from being abandoned and living on friends' floors to staying in hotel rooms the size of houses. But everything he did was for me.

PaPâ encourages me to think that everything in life is a lesson. My PaPâ is psychology. My life is filled with lectures, psychology training, and high-pressure situations. It's controlled training, unlike what he faced. Lessons and in-the-moment situations. Micro-expressions and awareness training.

I like to compare our relationship to the relationship of Shawn Spencer and his dad Henry from the TV show Psych. If you know the show, you'll understand. We are connected. Wherever we go, I memorize my surroundings, create a moment to hyper-focus on details that no one else sees, and, like the show, he asks me how many hats are in the room.

Then we study micro-expressions. I'm expected to learn and memorize people's faces, read their emotions, and understand if they are being honest or trying to pull one over on me without saying a single word. PaPâ encourages me and makes me feel I can do anything.

Why do we do this? Why does he teach this way? You'll soon see. Some moments will be hard to believe. You'll be surprised at others. And some you may not even understand right away, but keep reading; by the end, it all makes sense.

He found something special, a different path. Unlike the TV shows we watch that have been dramatized, the words in this book are true. If anything, they are toned down. Read away if you want to see why I'm so proud of my PaPâ.

You should read this book because it is good and will help you.

I feel this book can help everyone. Reading this book is important to learn how business connects with psychology. But even more than so, this book is about connections. Connecting with friends, family, and colleagues, and how business and wealth aren't everything.

Success is different for each person. This book explains how you should find your own happiness rather than what is expected.

Enjoy the read,

Ren Thompson

Part One

"Sweet are the uses of adversity."

- William Shakespeare

LET'S GO

"Because I'm the person who decides if you have a job at the end of the day, that's why." This was the start of a consulting contract that would send my company value above ten million dollars and ultimately send us well above the hundred million dollar mark. The group, led by the Head of Marketing, challenged my new position.

"Why do we have to listen to you?" He asked.

I needed to make a play, one that would allow me to come out strong and quickly gain control of the room. This isn't too uncommon in the big leagues of business. I need to assert myself.

This may sound like a bold start, but with what I've faced and the adversities I've overcome, it's a tactic in psychology that allows me to disrupt a room. I assert the power to get things started. This is not my typical approach - I prefer a softer hand - but I've been in this situation before; ironically, this exact position.

So here I am, hired to analyze, rebuild, and create a more effective team with fewer employees and a smaller budget, and yet achieve higher results, not just in the margin, but in turnover.

But before I get too far ahead of myself, I should clarify.

This book isn't your average "business book." This isn't a "5-steps to success thing"; no, I do things differently. This is a new approach to learning, not always direct with answers, but slowly through the realization of my own experiences.

Hopefully, this approach can draw realizations in your life, teaching you about overcoming adversity, being dedicated to your goals, and ensuring you are charting the right course to guide you toward success.

Not the standard success the world teaches is the only path, but what YOU define as success. A method you chart toward YOUR SUCCESS.

In order to understand me, my approach, and the difference between what the world defines as success and YOUR SUCCESS, I'll need to take a step back.

This isn't your typical rags-to-riches story. It is a raw, unflinching account of my life, but it's much deeper than a memoir or autobiography. I was able to take misfortune and transform it into millions of dollars; ultimately discovering a different kind of success. MY SUCCESS.

Like most great stories, let's go back to the beginning. The challenging aspects of my life built me up like the movie Slumdog Millionaire. Discover how each experience builds me, teaches me, and prepares me to find the realizations that changed my life and hopefully can change yours.

There were big problems at school. The punks and the jocks were going at it like the Sharks and Jets. Trouble had been brewing for a while, and me and Jill getting together was the straw that broke the camel's back. It set off the entire school, so much so that police came into an assembly to quell the escalation.

But it didn't work, and things escalated even further. I was starting to get followed home from school.

A group of guys set this thing up to jump me after school when my best friend was away at a track meet. These guys, though, didn't know that I grew up in Yuma, Arizona, with the poor all fighting it out for the scraps. The violent crime rates in Yuma were thirty percent higher than the national average. And now I was in a farm town in Nevada? *Bring it on!*

These college-age kids passed me on the street in their van, driving back and forth, slowly. Finally, I threw my backpack down and put my hands up, like, "Let's go!"

The van stopped and six of them got out. They had baseball bats, but I had no weapons other than my fists and my mind. I felt I had no choice but to get into my fighting stance, and I started cracking my knuckles. I looked at them like a rabid dog: "Just so you know," I said, "one of you is going to die."

I cracked my knuckles again, the broken bones in my hand re-breaking in front of them. The sound was loud and the six guys with baseball bats could not *not* hear it, could not *not* hear my crazy.

I knew the only way to win this unwinnable fight was to use psychology, to make each one of them believe that they could very well be the one I kill. We all knew I couldn't take all six of them, but we also all knew that, before they got me, I could get at least one of them.

They started getting nervous. I could see it, the change in their body language, their hesitation, their backward steps. Then, all six of them and their baseball bats got back in their van and drove away.

This book is about me and my connections to people. But before I could learn how to connect, I had to learn how to survive. Sometimes that meant fighting. My upbringing was rough—yet it gave me the tools I use; now and every day. I am no longer a fighter but a connector, and I wouldn't be able to do what I can do today without having endured what I did along the way.

Before we get into business, we're going to start with me growing up in a hailstorm because it is from where we've come that we get to where we're going.

BROKEN DREAMS AND BASEBALL

My dad was a phenomenal athlete and was the best when it came to baseball. As a freshman in high school, he could throw ninety-five miles per hour, and he could do this left-handed. This was unheard of in the 80s, and he had the scouts drooling.

Baseball was the lone bright spot for my dad. He was the last of eleven brothers and sisters, and he faced an abusive childhood with his birth father as well as his stepfather. Catholic priests too. Drugs, alcohol, rape, and violence surrounded his daily life. Anything you can name, he pretty much faced it, so baseball was his escape, his way out. He could throw as hard as he wanted and release all his anger into that ball while building something that could give him a different future.

He'd just graduated high school and was going pro. The sky was the limit, his dream coming true before his eyes, so he and his buddies went out to celebrate over drinks. On the way back, they drove off the road and flew into a tree. The car wrapped around the arbor in an instant, and my dad's best friend died painfully in his arms.

It crushed my dad, giving him irreparable emotional damage. The accident also exacted a physical toll as his ankle was crushed by the engine—not to mention a massive concussion with likely life-long effects. He was still alive, thankfully, but he could no longer throw a baseball at ninety-five miles per hour. He never got to realize his dream, never got to "go pro." And he was *that* close.

However, he never lost his love for the game. Like Robert Redford in *The Natural* or Babe Ruth in real life, my dad went from pitcher to position player and continued to play on barnstorming semi-pro teams in Northern Nevada.

When he was still playing on these teams, he met my mom, they started dating, and one thing led to another. She would go see his games when I was still in her belly. She'd sit out in the bleachers, get some sun on her face and enjoy watching her man play ball.

One day, a flyball was hit out to center. My dad charged in and closed the gap on the arc before it fell to the grass. He rushed in and leapt into a dive. Falling onto his elbow, he made the catch!

In her recounting of this story, my mom tells how he remained on the ground longer than he normally does after a catch. He finally managed to get up and throw the ball back into the infield. Mom wasn't the only person who noticed; so did his team. The right fielder headed over and asked if he was okay.

"I'm fine," Dad said, but almost immediately, he began to wobble on his feet. Before the fielder could catch him, he fell to the ground, collapsed in a heap, and blacked out. Mom leapt off the bleachers and knew she had to do something, so she hoped into her car and drove it out onto the field. My dad's teammates lifted him into the car and mom sped off to the hospital.

"He's hurt," my mom told the E.R. as they arrived, "His stomach. Do something!"

Mom and Dad had just enough wherewithal to sign all the forms they needed to sign, and they got him to a back room for an x-ray.

The doctor came into the room and said something like, "We can't seem to get a good x-ray, it's blurry."

"Forget the x-ray, he's bleeding internally!" shouted my mom.

The doctor stopped, noticed my father's pale complexion, came to his senses, admitted that, indeed, that was a possibility, and ran some further tests.

Turns out, Mom was right. Dad had ruptured his spleen and was losing all sorts of blood. They got him prepped to remove the spleen, but, suddenly, he died on the table. He was, for all intents and purposes, dead, but they worked fast and managed to bring him back to life.

Fast forward to a year later, and Dad gets called into the office at work, where the guy in the suit confronts him: "Hey, so you gave blood in our last blood drive?"

"Yeah."

"That's illegal. You tested positive for hepatitis. You can't be doing that, and you were supposed to report this to the company." Dad objected, telling them that he didn't have it and that he doesn't know what was going on.

Later that day, when he got home from work, he told my mom. This sparked a fervent investigation from Mom and Dad, who did some digging in the form of phone calls to the hospital. They forensically searched the house for any type of receipt, but they couldn't find one. Come to think of it, they never remembered having received one! As a result, my parents went into the hospital to talk to the brass.

"I'm sorry," they said, "there's no record of us having treated your husband as a patient."

Mom almost lost it. She recounted how she drove him there from the ballfield, and how there were witnesses to that: "I can tell you which doctors and nurses we saw!" she yelled, getting frustrated and angry.

They refused to budge. Mom - juggling three kids - and Dad fought for answers that the suits didn't want to give. They persisted, and after a few more visits, it came to light that they gave my dad a blood transfusion when they operated on his spleen and that, astonishingly, the blood they gave him was not clean.

The hospital gave my father hepatitis and then denied the whole thing, saying that my dad had never walked into the hospital that day.

The hospital didn't want to get sued, and my parents were poor so they couldn't afford the lawyers to take them to court. And so that is the way it was.

I don't think life should be like that.

You can treat hepatitis today, but that was not possible back in the 80s. They said my dad would "be lucky to live five years."

I was about to be born, about to come into this world, and my dad had just received a death sentence. I don't think life should be this way either.

To compound matters further, he went from being a rockstar employee for the area power company to having to scrape by on disability. This prevented him from working in the traditional way. Still, my dad kept fighting for his life, doing different tests, keeping in shape, and doing all that he could.

He became all about "mind over matter." His body was failing him, but he could still keep his mind sharp, and control what he could. It rubbed off on me, and is best typified by one of his mantras: "If you can put your mind to it, you can do anything."

I think life should be *this* way—mind over matter.

Though I came into the world as my father was already on his way out, he showed me so much. Taught me so much, and he loved me so much, in his own way.

I don't have many memories earlier than about age 14, but this is one of them. When I was three years old, my dad took me to the doctor with him. Somehow, I remember, or maybe I remember Dad's later retelling of the story. I'm not sure, but what I know is that the doctor told my dad that the disease had eaten through almost his entire liver, and "you are going to die within the year."

My dad mind-over-mattered it that whole year, and three hundred and sixty-five days later, we went back in for his checkup—maybe just so they could tell him he was dead. But, to our joyous, overwhelming relief, they don't. They tell him that his body has "responded," that his body is actually growing another liver.

The doctors are amazed. Like us, they don't believe it. But because my dad did believe that if he adopted the right mindset he could beat his illness, he was still alive. My dad *is* strength. My dad is my hero, and I sometimes still see him sleeping with his eyes open because that's how he survived his siblings chasing him around with axes and such when he was younger. He had a bad childhood, and so he tried his best to make sure mine wasn't awful. He tried - he did - but mine still wasn't very good.

Even as a youngster, I absorbed what the world was telling me about my father. He wasn't going to be around forever, and maybe even not for that much longer. His disease made him feel like he had the flu every day of his life, and some days were worse than others. If it was a really bad day for him, I'd just lay in bed with him all day and watch movies (I'm still a pretty big movie buff because of it).

He was told, "You are going to die this year," year after year, for 16 years.

In his short time, he made sure to teach me as much as he could, which he did in his own unique way. But in some respects, I owe much of who I am - what I've learned - to that incredibly strong man who was my father.

One day, when I was about seven, he took me to a relative's house—I'd never been there before. This house was nothing short of a heroin den, and he had brought me here because he wanted me to "start learning" about people, to gain the ability to read them.

"Stand in the middle of this room," he told me, my eyes wide, "and tell me who is going to freak out from their high."

My schoolwork that day was to stand in the middle of a drug house and watch my family members shoot up with heroin. I was to do this so I could begin to see who going to be dangerous, and who was going to be a problem.

It was D.A.R.E. on another level. It was real-life education, and I was 7. Of course, we never told my mom about it.

And the life lessons kept coming. Though Pops never went to college and had nothing resembling a Ph.D., he was training me in psychology as a 7-year-old. I remember the lessons. They've stuck around, and as a result, I developed a way to internalize and relate to people as if I went through their experiences myself. My dad was dying, and he was passing on to me how to live—and how to help others live.

Now, I was nine years old: "I need you to promise me that you will never touch drugs or alcohol," Dad said to me, "until you are married and have your own house and career— then the choice is yours."

"I promise, Dad. But only if you stay alive until I graduate high school."

I started playing baseball because that was another thing my dad taught me. I was his son, and it came to fruition that I had his gift. I could hurl a baseball, fast, and with precision. By the time I was a freshman in high school, I was throwing ninety-plus miles per hour. Baseball was my ticket. Baseball was life. We'd be driving across town in his truck and Dad would hit me with a situation: "Alright, Billy—runners on first and third, bottom of the last inning, up by one run. One out. You're playing shortstop. A groundball is hit hard at you, one step to your left. What do you do?"

"Turn two. End the game." I'd say with confidence, these scenarios drilled into me.

He would tell me that I was correct, and we would drive on down the road. Baseball was everything. I practiced all the time and came to know that I was better than my peers. I was getting noticed, getting attention, to the extent that there were whispers of a Major League career—I could have the dream that was ripped from my father. Things would be set right.

Growing up in the struggling life of poverty, my baseball career was the one thing that could bring our family together. It was amazing how my family would attend all my games, be together and not argue, not fight or stress, and just enjoy watching me play. It made me want to try even harder.

In high school, I was throwing shutouts and hitting home runs, and things were good. Then, at a year-end game, I strode to the plate. On the first pitch, I swung hard and connected.

The ball connected with my bat, compressed, and flew off with a crack. I sent it arcing out toward left-center field. It hit the top of the fence and I was digging for second. Then, I turned on the burners and headed for third.

"Get down!" my third base coach yelled.

I dove into third base headfirst, Pete Rose style, hard, with all the grit of Charlie Hustle himself. But as I was in the air, I realized I'd come in too hot. I thought, *Oh crap, I'm too close to the bag!*

I tried to recoil my arms, but my right arm, my pitching arm, wrapped awkwardly around the bag. I heard the pop and felt the tear in my shoulder. And, even at 14, my heart sank to the floor as I knew in an instant that my pitching career was done. I would not play Major League baseball.

This was so scary to me because I had no backup plan. I had placed all of my eggs in the basket labeled "Baseball." To a young me, the writing was on the wall, baseball was over.

Life is unfair in poverty. When you grow up with the generational struggles of never having money, you don't get what I've now come to think of as "normal" within the realm of the "Pursuit of Happiness." In poverty, you don't get even the essentials—so when my arm was torn, I didn't get surgery; it wasn't an option. Nope, I got a sling and a "good luck."

If we'd had money or even just slightly better insurance, the ligaments in my shoulder could have easily been repaired. I was young and could have gotten back to strength, taken the mound again, and pursued my childhood dream. But nope. That wasn't in the cards of the hand I'd been dealt.

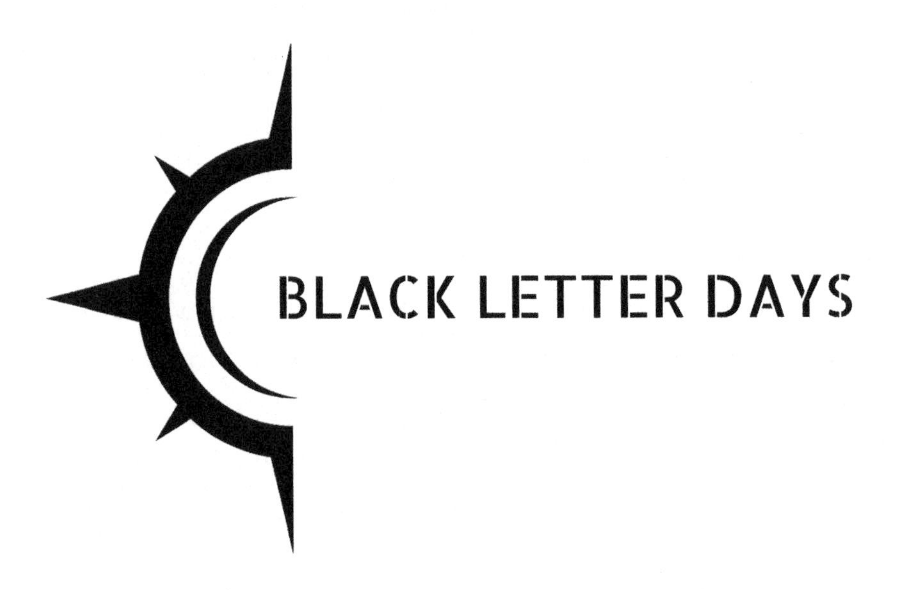

BLACK LETTER DAYS

Though I didn't realize it at the time, Dad had given me a lot more than just a flamethrowing arm. He'd been teaching me lessons from the school of hard knocks since I could walk. He was always picking up these oddball jobs - painting houses, doing yard work, being a janitor - anything he could get paid "under the table" to do to help us out.

It still wasn't enough though. I had to help, had to carry my weight. I remember coming home from the fourth grade, right before Christmas break. My mom is an amazing baker, and I saw that she was making dozens upon dozens of cookies. At first, I was excited because I thought they were for me. But they were not, they were *capital.*

My dad told me to load all the tins of cookies into the car. Then, dad and I hopped in and drove over to the rich part of town.

"Here's the deal, Billy," he told me en-route, "we don't have enough money to pay rent. Plus, we can't even afford any presents for you and your sisters. There is no Santa Claus."

"What?"

I said, like a fundamental truth has just been ripped from me.

"Yeah, Santa is a lie. Sorry, but we have to sell these cookies so your sisters can have presents. As a grown adult, I can't walk around door-to-door like you. You're a kid, it'll work better if you do it."

"Do what?" I asked, confused.

"Walk around this neighborhood and sell these tins of cookies for twenty-five dollars a pop to all the people in these big houses." He told me, matter-of-factly.

"Huh?"

"You can do this. In fact, you *have* to if you want to help your family and make Christmas possible. Your mom worked all day, then came home to bake everything, and I wish I could do this for you, but I am here to teach you how to. I believe in you, son. Trust me, you can do this." His faith in me inspired me. Everything my dad did involved a lesson, some test, or a challenge like this, all with the aim to teach me about people and the world. A lot of psychology, in real-time, and pretty much anything dad asked of me, I did.

So, I grabbed a tin and walked up to the nearest, biggest house. I knocked on the door and when it opened, I smiled sweetly and hinted at our plight, sold the tray of cookies, put the twenty-five dollars in my pocket, and walked back to my dad in the car.

I gave him the money. He nodded and gave me another tin of fresh-baked cookies to sell to some rich people. I went up to another big house, rang the doorbell, and sold that one too. This time, even quicker. Then another house. Another. I was honing my pitch and slinging those cookies faster than any Santa could've eaten them.

At the end of the night, I'd sold all the tins and my family paid the rent that December. My sisters even got to open a couple of presents on Christmas morning.

I'd just received my first lesson in sales. I made my dad proud and knew I was good at it.

MY SUCCESS that night gave my parents an obvious idea, so, Mom kept baking—expanding to cinnamon rolls, pastries, brownies… anything, and then Dad and I would roll up with our Tupperware all over town, selling them individually for 2 or 3 bucks a pop. This improved our family's life, so I wanted to sell as often as possible.

Even as a grade-schooler, I was starting to learn how to work the room, how to read people, and how to use psychology to improve my life.

It helped in other ways too. I was always changing schools. I ended up going to four different high schools, first in Arizona, then California, then Nevada. I'd get home from school one day and my parents would be like, "Billy, we're moving."

"When?"

"Tomorrow."

The reasons were usually because we couldn't afford rent, or we wanted to get away from or closer to some member of the family. Sometimes it was to get away from one of my dad's mistresses (a bad habit he had—even more painful when it would turn out to be one of my mom's best friends). Most of the time, I feel we moved because we were poor, and the grass was always greener somewhere else. I had to say goodbye to a lot of friends and then work on making new ones. To survive, I had to sell. I had to sell myself, and I had to do it a lot on my own.

I went to five or six different primary schools and four different high schools. It was an atypical schooling—but such a valuable education.

My parent's marriage was awful. My dad was a great father, but he was a terrible husband. He just did not know how to love. Being a parent came naturally to him, and he was great, but being a husband just did not (the guy could make *any* woman like him, with a look, in a second. It was amazing. Mom didn't like it so much). And through his own struggles, he would get drunk. He was a great dad, but he was definitely an alcoholic.

He had this extreme paranoia about him too, and once you put alcohol and drugs into the mix, it was not good.

My mother was loving and gave it her all, but with the life she was handed (generational struggles), she also struggled to give the picture-perfect childhood she wanted for her kids.

Mom, like Dad, faced endless tragedies—a challenging childhood that, still to this day, I don't know all the details of. I do know that on her path to breaking the mold, her first love - her high school sweetheart - was killed in a car accident. She was left to face this pain alone, then with no support and a terrible home life, she found herself pregnant at 16.

Her family kicked her out of the home and left her to survive alone. When she met my father, she already had a toddler and he'd already been to hell and back. But through these tragedies, she was the most caring person in the world, so much so that it became a detriment, with more and more people taking advantage of her throughout her life. So much love to give, but not enough given back to her, and that tends to break us down. Even through all that Mom faced, she's still an amazing, and deeply caring person.

I suppose you could say that my parents - two people with issues stemming from their childhood, with zero support, facing the life they were given - did the best they could for me. I appreciate everything they did.

I do have some good memories from childhood, but mostly they exist as small islands in a sea of bad.

I remember reading a book once called *Night of the Twisters*. It was the story of a little boy and his family—how a series of tornadoes dropped from the sky one day and they lost everything. The book explained the comparison between a red-letter day and a black-letter day; depending on the news, it would either be good news with a red-letter or bad news with a black-letter. It was such a big deal to the boy in the book.

I didn't quite get it though. Every day seemed like a Black-Letter Day for me. Tornadoes came often, and they came with great ferocity.

So, why have I told you about my dad, my mom, and the nature of my upbringing? Have I done it to create sympathy, to make you like me and relate to me? Well, that would be a failed objective from the outset. My experiences are uniquely mine, and whilst you may be able to draw parallels, or you are observing a scenario you may never have encountered, my experiences are different from all of yours, irrespective of the similarities. I'm not saying that they are better, or worse, they are just different.

However, what we can have in common is how we use our upbringings and react to them. Use them as a source of strength. Remember your origins; there are countless lessons to be taken from these. Do not hide behind them or use them as an excuse. Extract the value from them and use them to propel you forward. In this example, I experience my first taste of marketing and selling from my dad, which all came about as a result of his prior tribulations.

In the greatest adversity, there is strength and wisdom to be found.

A BIRTHDAY AFTERNOON

In the fifth grade, I was at home with my dad. This guy showed up at the door out of the blue. He was haggard. Even at 10 years old, I could already tell he was a druggie.

Turned out, it was my dad's brother, one of his ten siblings. I'd never seen the guy.

My dad said something like, "Haven't seen you in a long time…"

My dad's brother - my uncle I guess - said he wanted to take me out for my birthday.

Oh yeah, it's my birthday!

He said he "just knew" it was my birthday, and he wanted to take me out for the afternoon.

He didn't have a car or anything, and he was in a bad way, but my dad agreed to allow him to walk me to McDonald's; hey, one less meal Pops would have to buy.

He was fine with it, but I look at this guy and *I'm* not too sure. I could tell he was anxious; I could read physical and emotional pain in the micro-expression on his face. People with these tells, like an abused pit bull, I knew even back then, could be dangerous.

Still, McDonald's *was* McDonald's, and I wasn't going to pass it up. He even said I could get a toy.

I got laced up and ready to go and we walked out the door. I waved goodbye to my dad and embarked on a walk with his brother whom I never knew existed.

We started walking, the conversation pretty quiet at first. I wanted him to feel comfortable, so I started asking him a lot of questions. At this age, I was already capable of reading adults, understanding their personality traits, and how to get people to open up.

He started giving answers, short at first but getting longer with each one. Then the faucet turned on and he just started opening up and sharing all these things about his life. He was telling stories and filling in blanks and we were just shooting the breeze like old buds. I could see his spirits lifting and before long we were walking into McDonald's. We joked around in line and ordered our food. I got to pick out my toy. Then we sat down and spent a couple of hours eating and playing and hanging out.

When we finally left, we talked all the way home on the walk back. When we got to my house, he gave me a hug. He wished me "happy birthday" one last time and thanked me for spending some time with him.

Then, I watched him walk away.

Shortly after this visit, I found out that he committed suicide.

It was really hard. It was tough. But I was really glad my uncle chose to come over that day. It was great to get to meet him, to spend my birthday with him. I hope I had a positive effect on him in his last days. I think I did. I hope I did. I wish I could have done more. But maybe I was at least able to be an island of good in his sea of bad? Even if just for one afternoon.

Part Two

"If I give up now, I'm going to regret it."

- Monkey D. Luffy – One Piece

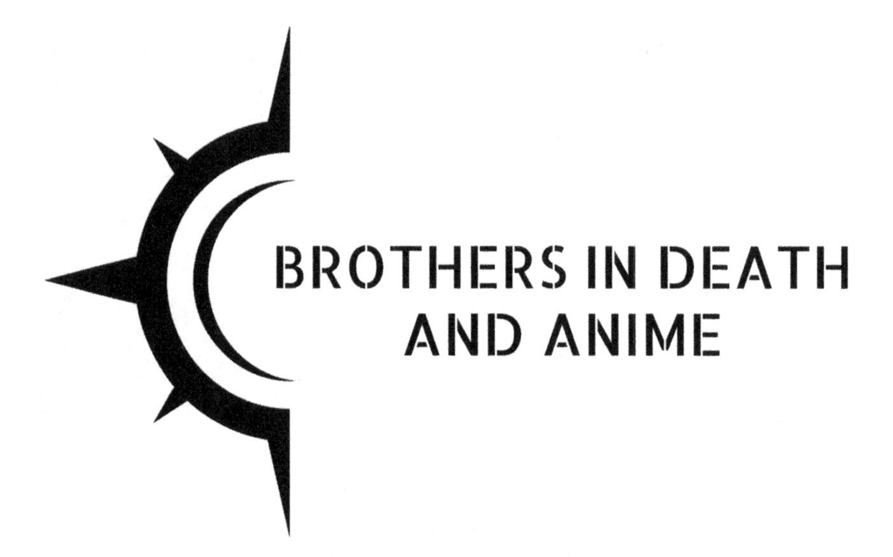

BROTHERS IN DEATH AND ANIME

So, after I tore my shoulder diving into third base and finished up my freshman year in California, it was time to move again.

"Where are we going this time?" I asked my mom.

"Fallon," she said.

"Where's that?"

"By Reno."

"Where's that?"

"Nevada."

When we arrived in Fallon I was greeted with mixed feelings, what with having to start over and all. We pulled into town and arrived at our new home. I tentatively got out of the car and immediately the next-door neighbor's kid was eagerly walking toward us. He walked right up to me.

"My name is Mike," he said, with a big and welcoming smile, "You and I are now best friends."

Since the shoulder injury, I'd been lost without baseball. I had retreated inward and become highly introverted. This kid seemed like an angel or something."Okay," I replied, nodding.

We put up a basketball hoop, shot around, and played one-on-one all day every day. Mike was right, we were now best friends.

He brought me into the fold with his other best friend, Steve. We bonded quickly and became like brothers. Our trio was formed. We all came from similar backgrounds—drugs, violence, abuse, and the constant strains of poverty. We all knew we shared in the struggle, but the unique part was that we all wanted to break our generational cycles. We had this almost mystical bond, unspoken but agreed upon: we would escape our pre-fated lives, and we would do it together.

This brotherhood was one of those islands of good in the sea of bad. Mike, Steve, and I became inseparable. Plus, it turned out that Mike and Steve were some of the most popular kids in school, which gave me a huge leg up. Since I was their new best friend, I became popular by proxy. That year went by pretty well.

Then came summer vacation.

Mike and I had all these plans, all these things we were going to do. He thought he could get out of going to a family reunion in Utah and thought he could convince his parents to let him stay with me instead, but they made him go.

We said goodbye and were excited to see each other when he got back.

I recall being up in my sister's apartment (in the same complex as my parents) when I got a call from my mom.

"Billy, you have to come down here right now." The urgent tone of her voice told me that something was wrong. I rushed over and arrived at my house. I saw these two guys from the church where Mike, Steve, and I had been going. I saw them, their faces, using the skills that Dad had taught me. I knew in an instant that something bad has happened. My heart plummeted with the realization that it must be about Mike.

Mike's family reunion was held on a lake. There were jet skis, and it was on one of these that Mike had turned quickly to avoid a boat heading in the wrong direction; this brought him to a halt as the jet ski became waterlogged. His cousin was following closely behind and didn't see him in time. He simply didn't have time to avoid Mike, and he went right over the top of him. His jet ski collided at full speed with Mike's head.

It snapped his brainstem. He died instantly. My best friend Mike. Dead.

My island of good was gone, washed away by the sea of bad.

After they told me the news, I fell to my knees. I questioned God. I questioned everything. Losing my best friend made the pain too great for me to talk about with my dad; death was a demon from his past that he couldn't face, so it pulled us apart.

Steve shared my devastation. I didn't know how to act, how to be. It was almost too hard for us to be around each other during that time. I was used to dealing with adversity, to managing my emotions, but Mike's passing hurt. It hurt in ways that I struggled to comprehend, struggled to manage. It was like losing a part of me.

I pushed everything away—my dad, Steve, my family, and I retreated further inward. Life was too hard.

I was alone.

I finally got out of the house one day, needing a break from that day's newest family drama. I just started walking. I didn't know where I was going, I was adrift.

I stopped in front of a house. I seemed to recognize it, and, for some reason, it stopped my drifting. I looked up at the house and knew a guy named Kevin lived there. I didn't like Kevin. I could never tackle him on the football field, and he used to taunt me for it.

I'm not sure why, but I walked up and knocked on the door. Still can't pinpoint it—but maybe because he *wasn't* connected to me? Maybe because I wanted a fight. I don't know.

Kevin answered the door. I saw him and I looked at him with aggression, just because. But he looks at me with a true kindness in his eyes, which disarmed me, threw me off.

"Hey, I heard about Mike," he said, "are you okay?"

"No, I'm not okay," I said, seething, trying to relocate my rage.

"You wanna come inside?" he asked kindly.

I begrudgingly accepted and traipsed inside. All I could think was that I didn't like this kid. He was everything I wasn't. He was ripped, muscular, confident, and well-liked. He was perfect. I was not. So why was my rage fading away?

"Hey, I appreciate you being nice and all," I said, stiffening up once again looking for trouble, "but either you and I are going to be best friends, or we are going to be enemies."

Kevin took a long look at me, processing my awkward declaration in his head, shrugged, and said, "Okay then, let's be best friends."

I was taken aback. I kinda did want to fight him, but with Mike gone, I knew I could use another friend.

Kevin proceeded to tell me how he had to go to Philadelphia for a month with his family but that he was worried about me being alone with Mike's death still fresh in my mind. He asked me if I liked anime.

"I don't know what anime is," I told him.

He located a box of VHS tapes, "Just take this," he said, "They'll help."

With my best friend having just died and my newest friend leaving for a month, I retreated to my room and watched Japanese cartoons for a month straight. And you know what? They really did help. Somehow.

When Kevin came back, I had a new best friend. I missed Mike all the time, but I was beginning to understand that life was going to come with both backward and forward steps.

Sometimes, I didn't know when or how that next step forward would come—but connecting to people, I was finding, was key.

BEHIND THE FUTON

My dad was drinking more, drugs were becoming ever more prominent, and to make matters worse, my sisters were following suit. At this point, my mom was trapped in the middle, trying to hold things together but with no real way to corral the chaos, she couldn't prevent it..
Life was spiraling out of control.

At school, it was becoming a custom for my teachers to call Monday "Billy's Holiday" because they knew I would never show up. They'd come to learn that Monday was my day to rest, a day I needed to sleep and get my head right after dealing with a weekend of crazy at my house—all the drugs and fights and sirens, and an overall lack of stability, as I floated in that sea of bad searching for islands to grasp at.

On reflection, it was clear that my teachers adapted. I think they saw what I was caught up in as no choice or desire of my own. They started giving me more homework on Fridays, expecting me to show up Tuesday knowing what I had to know for the lesson.

In response, I worked hard and achieved good marks. I made some friends and a few enemies.

Kevin and I became inseparable, like Luffy and Zoro in the anime series *One Piece*—part of the same crew. We hung out 24/7. I needed to because Mom and Dad were fighting worse than normal—issues spiraling from the life they felt trapped in. History was repeating itself. They wanted away from drugs, alcohol, and violence, yet it had seeped in deep enough to become part of their daily lives.

They were trying to figure out how to help pull my sisters from the same mess, but Dad ran from his mental health by using drugs, alcohol, and women to block the pain.

One night, he shoved my mom hard and painfully. This was the first time he had ever done it, even with all the times they had fought. I tried to stop him, rushing at him in anger, but he simply caught me and threw me into the water cooler.

To this day, I cannot comprehend the amount of strength that man had, considering how sick he was.

And after a while, I didn't begrudge him for shoving me away. He didn't mean to hurt me, I know, he was just lost in the drugs and alcohol, and he couldn't handle the demons in his head anymore.

After that night, Dad wasn't around for a while. He was gone and Mom was done, done with everything. Life had continued to beat her down, leaving her with nothing. The endless stream of cheating, drug/alcohol abuse, rebellious children, and now the physical violence had brought her to an ending point, and, for a while, I felt like I lost my mother.

As an adult who understands a fair amount about psychology, it's heartbreaking for me to look back at what my mom faced. I realize the pain she was enduring, but at the time I was too young to understand, or even to help. There was nonstop and constant drama.

One night after school, I just couldn't face the thought of going home. I plain did not want to be there—if I was, I knew I was going to do something that would ruin my life. I called Kevin.

"You know my mom's rule," he told me after I begged to stay at his, "I can't have anyone over when she's not here."

I knew his mom was an x-ray technician at the hospital who worked late, and I also knew I was not supposed to go over when she was not home. But I couldn't bear the thought of going back to my house, not again. I loved my mom, but the issues at home were stacking up, and I was going to snap and do something stupid.

Still on the phone, I pleaded with Kevin. There was a futon tilted up against a back wall in his room, and he finally said I could come over and sleep behind it. I happily took the life raft.

I ran over, he snuck me upstairs, and I stayed the night.

And then, I just kept staying the night. I started living between a futon and a wall, and my life felt perpetually caught between a rock and a hard place.

We kept it up for a few weeks, and amazingly Kevin's mom hadn't caught on. We managed to keep a routine that keeps me hidden. One night, though, she crept up the stairs and surprised us. She looked around and put two and two together.

"What are you doing?!" she asked me.

"I can't go home," I said, "Please—please don't make me."

She must have seen something in my eye; something serious, something grave. I knew this because her look softened a little, and she walked downstairs and drove over to my house.

She wasn't gone long. I was nervous as she came into the room.

"Billy," she said calmly, "you can stay here as long as you want."

To this day I don't know exactly what she saw, but I do know what she observed—a sea of bad. She saw the chance to be an island of good.

MY JILL

It's just me, Kevin, his sister, Sydney, and his mom, Cheryl, and we created this really cool situation. I bonded with his little sister right away and seemed to add some muse to the family. Cheryl said more than once how I became like some "missing link".

It was an island of heaven.

Even getting yelled at by Cheryl to "clean this up," or "do this or you're grounded" was great. I loved that too.

Things went well for a while, but just like always in my young life, it felt like just enough to taste but not enough to be satisfied. At the same time, there had always been this optimistic side that gnaws at me. Maybe it was the miracles my dad showed me that kept me feeling like anything was possible. I really hoped this new life I was living could be permanent, but that wouldn't be possible until I built it myself.

Living at Kevin's was a second chance, a rebirth, a new world. Plus, Kevin decided he wanted to make a movie.

Yep, he had a camera and he convinced me that we should write a script and shoot the thing. Why not, right?

To get more writing time, I convinced Kevin to switch classes out of Calculus and into my Personal Finance class. Looking back, I feel a little sorry for the teacher because in the middle of class, right in the middle of her lesson on balancing a checkbook, Kevin would be writing a scene and he'd finish it and toss the notebook over to my desk with a flop. Then I'd write my scene, building off what Kevin had just written. That's how we did it. Team writing. To the chagrin of Mrs. Goings, we finished our script for *Rival Schools.*

The screenplay was written, and it was time for casting. A lot of people thought we were crazy, foolish, or stupid, but others were kind of intrigued. Kevin took some auditions and got a commitment from one of the girls in his class.

But she was a terrible actress. I mean, none of us could act, but this girl was *bad.* After a couple of rehearsals, she knew it too. She looked at Kevin after a take and simply said, "Why don't you try my friend, Jill?"

I hear the name. "Jill." A memory is triggered: Jill from Spanish class, last year. She was amazing. She was lovely. I loved her the moment I saw her. Jill. My mind flashed me back to the day we were taking a make-up test together out in the hallway; she leaned over after a question and put her head on my lap.

"Hey, I can see up your nose," she said, funny, quirky, lovely.

I stood up abruptly. I liked her so much in that awkward teenage way that I could barely even talk to her, let alone come into physical contact with her. So, when she put her head on my lap, I shot up onto my feet and her head hit the ground.

Awkward.

I wanted that moment back. I wanted to be able to talk to this girl. I wanted to get to know this girl. I *needed* to get to know this girl.

Jill.

I heard her name and remembered that there was a kissing scene in the movie. "Yes!" I said, eagerly. "Get Jill!"

Kevin spoke to Jill, and she agreed to be in our little movie. We hadn't started filming yet, but she started hanging out with us as we planned final shoots and takes. Jill and I picked up right where we left off in Spanish class. We liked each other, liked being around each other. We flirted and made excuses to spend time together.

But she was in a committed relationship. Plus, she was a senior and I was still only a junior. But I loved her. I *already* loved her—and I think she knew I did.

With this backdrop, I'll take you to one evening at Kevin's house. The phone rang, and it was for me: the police are at my house. My sister's boyfriend had been beating her, again. I hung up the phone and looked into Kevin's eyes.

"I'm going to kill him. I am going to kill my sister's boyfriend." Rage was building up inside me. Kevin knew that rage.

"Yeah," said Kevin slowly, "you can't do that, Billy."

I didn't agree with my friend. I walked outside, fuming, and started taking furious swings at the air.

"I'm gonna kill him," I said on repeat.

Kevin had followed me outside. He knew I was probably capable, but he told me again that I was not going to do that, that I was not going to "Throw away your life by doing that."

I was not thinking about my future. I was not thinking about all the trouble I would obviously get into if I followed through on my plan. I thought of nothing but killing the man who had been beating my sister.

As my rage built, logic and reasoning abandoned me, and I started punching a stucco wall with my fists. I was beyond furious; so enraged, so fed up with my life and wanting to take it out on a bad person; someone who I felt deserved it. I hit the wall over and over and over, bloodying it up with my hands. The bones in my hand were breaking, but I liked the pain, so I kept hammering that stucco wall and amping myself up to go kill someone.

Then, there she was. Not my sister—Jill. She just appeared around the back wall and was there.

I saw her out of the corner of my eye, and I didn't know why she was there, but I really didn't want her to be. This spurred me on further, and the compounded misery of the girl I love seeing this part of me added to my rage. I continued to go at the wall with my bloodied and broken fists, but that wasn't doing it for me anymore. I walked over to the nearby steel wall as if the stucco wasn't hard enough to break me.

My hands were as swollen as two softballs as I kept pounding the steel. You could hear the bones breaking, but I kept going. I wanted more. I was wild and enraged, crazy-eyed, in so much pain, and wanting to dish out this pain to someone or something else. Jill walked over to me.

"You need to stop, Billy," she said calmly.

"I can't!"

She stepped between me and the wall. I raised my fist again, ready to continue to punch the wall because of the sick pleasure-pain it was giving me. Jill crossed her arms and looked at me with about the most serious and humanly raw look you could imagine. "I'm not going to move," she said, "If you take another swing, all you're going to hit is me."

I screamed out some sort of primal roar. I didn't want to stop breaking my bones and bloodying up my skin, but I couldn't risk hitting Jill. I looked into her eyes; they said more than any words had ever said to me in my entire life. I put my hands down, and she wrapped her arms around me, holding me tight.

On that day, I knew Jill would someday be my wife.

Psychology teaches us that trauma has many different lasting forms. One of these is the feeling of not deserving happiness in life. As a child who faced trauma, it can leave deep emotional scars. This can create a warped view of oneself. This leads to fear of recreating this trauma or even self-blame. This can result in muddled emotions that make the person feel they do not deserve happiness or prevent them from wanting to peruse happiness. Working on yourself to find a resolution can be hard. If you find that you are the type to impose self-criticism, remember to analyze the situation, good and bad, and reflect on the lessons learned. Understand that you are not perfect, but that you do deserve happiness. Realize that you were doing the best you could do at that moment. Learn from it and move forward with this new experience.

Practice thinking and saying to yourself. "I deserve to be happy." This may seem simple, it will take some time and effort, and won't come instantly, but it works. As you continue to remind yourself that you are worth it, that you deserve to be happy, and other positive declarations, you will begin to change the narrative of your own life.

DEATH AND LOVE

My hands and fingers still flex, still work, somehow, despite all the traumatic shattering I've put them through. They just crack all the time, and not quietly. They are a constant reminder of the pain I had given myself because of the pain I've absorbed from others.

More pain came when I needed to move on once more. My time at Kevin's was a swift, yet a much-needed reprieve. It may have just saved my life, and I was incredibly thankful for that, but then Cheryl met the love of her life, Jay. I knew from day one that Jay was going to be there for the long run. He loved Cheryl, Kevin, and Sydney, and I wasn't going to let myself get in the way. I wasn't going to let my baggage get in the way of their future.

I moved back home.

I always knew the move back home was inevitable, but this didn't make it any easier. Through living with Kevin for those few short months, I had finally started to gain some goodness in my life, some consistency. But like all of the islands of good, it was fleeting, and then it was back to floating in that sea of bad. I had to go back to the

house where pain, stress, and my mental health would be tested daily, and hourly. I felt alone again like no one could see me.
The difference this time, though, was Jill.

On one spring evening, Jill and I were walking through the park. We were walking through the trees and talking when she told me again that she had to stay with her current boyfriend "*forever*," which was what she had been taught. They'd been dating for over a year, and it was what everyone was expecting from her. On top of that, she thought she loved him.

"Just because you love someone," I told her, "it doesn't mean you have to be with them." Mike used to say that.

Jill was quiet for a bit. When she eventually spoke again, she went on to explain how her family wouldn't see it that way.

In response, I told her that there is more than one way to live a life. In a thinly veiled reference to myself, I hinted strongly that other people cared about her, and would take care of her. We went on to have a great talk, a real intimate thing, an opening up of who we were and what we wanted. We hugged and said goodbye, and when I left the park alone, I decided to meet up with Kevin.

In true teenage boy fashion, I told him all about our walk in the park and our awesome talk. Kevin reminded me again how her boyfriend was a popular kid, the most popular in the punk clique. I was a jock. Kevin could cross through the social boundaries of high school, but I couldn't.

"Look," he told me, "if you go and try to date Jill, you're going to catch a lot of heat. This guy's gonna come at you."

I told him again how I felt about Jill, how I just *knew*.

"I have to do this," I said, and Kevin reluctantly agreed. He always had my back, even against his better judgment.

A few days went by, and Jill and I were hanging out, flirting, and secretly trying to hold hands without anyone noticing. One day, she had to go to the movies with her boyfriend and somehow convinced me to go along.

It wasn't good. From the outset, it was like he knew something was up, talking about how "if I ever saw anyone fooling with "my girl," I'd beat the hell out of him."

He was a tough kid, sure, but at that point in my life, I was hitting walls for pleasure—what was this guy gonna do?

We somehow survived the movie and a few hours later, I met up with Jill and she was crying: "It's over with me and my boyfriend," she said through tears.

I pulled her in, holding her close, and we headed straight to my house. No one cared if I brought a girl home; the house was an open field. I took to her to my room, and consoled her, trying anything I can to make her feel better. She looked at me with glistening tears magnifying her big beautiful brown eyes, and she slowly moved in. My first kiss with Jill was soggy, wet, but perfect, and we spent the night together. The next day we woke up together and, for the first time, we spent the whole day together, just running around town, holdings hands, and reveling in each other's company.

Jill graduated high school, and was looking to start at a local college but didn't really know what to do, knowing she would have trouble affording housing and tuition. Meanwhile, I still had one more year of high school.

"Don't worry about it," I told her, "I'll get a job and find a place. We can stay at my dad's in the meantime, and I'll somehow figure out all my school stuff. We'll do it."

Right before we were set to implement our plan, I was still at home, and I'm trying to find that island of good in this wide sea of bad.

Against this backdrop, I received a call from my dad one night.

"Hey," he said, "I just wanted to call and tell you I love you and say goodbye." He then went on to tell me how he felt confident that I had found the right woman in Jill, that I would "be okay."

And then he told me that he'd just taken an entire bottle of OxyContin.

"Go to the hospital and get your stomach pumped!" I pleaded with him, panic rising in my chest and pouring out of me.

But he didn't want to, and I had to work hard, pleading and begging, to get him to go.

"Okay," he said finally, and he assured me that he was going to the hospital. Relief replaced the panic, but I was anxious and filled with trepidation. I wasn't sure that I fully believed him.

We said a rushed goodbye and hung up the phone.

He did go to the hospital; I think mostly because I asked him to. He made it there to get his stomach pumped. But it was too late.

The OxyContin was deep in his body, and whatever the hospital gave him to counteract it had the opposite effect. One minute, he was standing there flirting with the nurse. The next, he fell silent, and his heart stopped. My anxiety and trepidation were well-founded.

My dad was dead. The death certificate says suicide.

When my sister called to tell me, I remember going numb. It took several minutes for the message to sink in, for my anxiety to be replaced by a flood of overwhelming grief.

I couldn't believe it, and I couldn't imagine my life without him. My love for my dad and my relationship with him was one of the few constants in my life. One of my islands. Without it, I wanted my life to end. Nothing was what it should be any longer, and I had that all too familiar feeling that life shouldn't be like this.

The pain was so deep, so vivid, but I couldn't shed a single tear. It was all pain; a mind-numbing pain that strips away the body's ability to do anything. I suffered emotional damage that would never heal, and a pain that made me want to rip apart the skin from my flesh.

At such an impressionable age, I found myself lost; my father was gone, and with him, I lost my mentor, my friend, and my confidant. I was 16, and I no longer had a dad. I was left alone, again. This pain set me too far out to sea that I could no longer see any islands in the distance. I had no hope, nothing but darkness as I began to sink, allowing myself to drown.

I remember thinking, "I'm done." Life sucks. What was the point of being good all this time? Never breaking a rule never made anything better. I decided that I was going to *burn the world down* because nothing good ever happened to me when I was playing the good guy. I'm going to become the bad guy.

I was ready and primed to unleash hellfire, but then Jill came over. Someone had called her, told her, and she came to me. She calmed me down and helped me breathe; she helped me process.

She was an angel. The love I had for this woman broke through to outshine all of the hatred that was swelling in my gut. I had the thought that if I was going to throw away my life, I guess I would at least try to fix hers first. I reasoned that if and when she got tired of me and left, *then* I could burn the world down, but before I sabotaged my life, I could help this woman I loved. I could help her escape so she could have anything but a life of pain.

I would build a life that defied our heritage.

Part Three

"If you are not willing to learn, no one can help you. If you are determined to learn, no one can stop you."

-Zig Ziglar

INTO BUSINESS

My dad was dead. My mom, at 40, found out she was pregnant. Everything was upside down. Except, that is, except for Jill. I needed her, and I knew it, so I resolved to give her everything I had. By this point, we had only been dating for a couple of months, but I was all in. I got to know her parents, and they made an attempt of accepting me, but it didn't feel real.

Look at me, look at my past, I remember thinking, *who would accept me?* I was a young victim of impostor syndrome, and at that age, it was hard for me to relate to anyone—it felt to me as though most people had never experienced any real tragedy in their life. To my young mind, I justifiably believed that I'd endured more than most people face in an entire lifetime and I'd only been around for 16 years. Life was moving fast; I couldn't seem to slow it down. It felt like barely a moment has passed, yet at the same time, it was like Jill and I had been together for years.

After only a few months of being together, Jill and I stood in front of Jill's parents in their living room attempting to tell them about the seriousness of our relationship. We were just kids, but I stood up for what Jill and I had.

I confidently told Jill's dad that I loved his daughter and that she loved me. I told him about the apartment we had lined up in Reno.

He looked me in the eye, sternly, "Are you sitting here trying to tell me that you're ready for marriage? That you can take care of my daughter for the rest of her life?"

I confidently met his gaze, "I know beyond a shadow of a doubt that this is my girl for the rest of my life. I will take care of her."

We almost entered into a negotiation, her parents trying to get the measure of me and me desperate to prove to them that our love was real and that I could look after her. At one point, our plans were referred to as "a mistake." All I heard was, "I'm not good enough."

That's fine, I thought, *more fuel.* At this point in my life, I had begun to learn how to use my past as fuel and motivation—a skill that would go on to define MY SUCCESS and serve me well throughout my life and career. I have the ability to recall the pain of my past but instead of allowing it to derail me, I use it as fuel to drive me forward and hone my focus.

Using this skill, I taught myself that I could handle this situation, positively. In the end, Jill and I moved to Reno together.

Habits are formed when something triggers an action. That action may cause a sense of gratification, which triggers a release of dopamine, meaning that we are likely to take that action again when the trigger presents one more. This cycle, when repeated forms a habit.

Let's look at a small habit, like biting our nails. Many people habitually bite their nails. Why is this? It is because, at a young age, we may have experienced stress, and in response, we may have nervously bitten our nails. This action led to a sense of comfort, which reduced the stress and made us feel good. As a result, because we felt good, we repeated that action the next time we felt stressed. We repeat this process again and again to the point where it feels normal, and a habit is formed.

In my late teens, the habit that I had learned, when that made me feel better, was using my struggles as fuel. It changed my perspective, turned suffering into strength, and it felt good. It felt good because, when I did that, it created success and I used it to achieve my goals.

To this effect, I believe that success is a habit. After all, success feels good, right? We can become addicted to that feeling of success. It is something that salespeople and marketers know well, and it leads to repeating the practices that work for us. I, like many others, have created a habit of success, and I have become self-sufficient; using my own energy to achieve this.

And the great thing is that anybody can do this. All it requires is the mindset. It requires a mindset that overturns and throws away the instinct to be the victim and instead converts victimhood into rocket fuel. This is power, this is motivation, and this is how the disenfranchised and the disadvantaged turn hardship into success.

It's within your power.

Jill and I embarked eagerly and optimistically into our bright new future. Only, and I'm sure many of you reading this will not be surprised, our teenage dreams were tinged with idealistic optimism, and our new future was not as simple as we'd believed.

When Jill and I moved in together, things didn't get any easier. Now, I needed to take care of us, but I was only 16 years old, about to turn 17, and no one would hire me. Things were tough. We were together and on our own, but we needed to find some money fast. Fortunately, Mom was incredibly supportive of Jill and me in a time when few accepted us. A couple of weeks after we moved out, she came and visited us for my birthday.

"What do you want for your present?" she asked.

"I just want some food," I said, hungry, broke, "Take me to the grocery store?"

She agreed and we headed to the grocery store to put some food in my pantry. Mom and I filled up the cart and stood in line to check out. All I can think of, looking at the cart full of food, was how hungry I was. I just wanted to go home and cook, but the line was long and was taking forever. I looked upfront and there were no courtesy clerks to bag the groceries.

Using my pain as motivation, I figured I'd hurry up the process. I walked up front and started putting people's food in bags. First one customer and then I started with the next person. The checker was all smiles, and I was really hustling. The work made the wait pass faster, and decreased the time until I could eat something. I could almost taste the home-cooked ham and eggs as I'm shoved items into plastic bags like it's Level Eight on Tetris.

After the second customer, I'd gained the attention of the manager, who walked over and stopped, arms crossed, looking at me go. I looked up and saw him looking at me but kept on bagging up the groceries. He approached me.

"Hey," he said, "do you want a job?"

I stopped and looked at him, almost in awe and eagerly nodded, "Yes!"

I began my first job as a courtesy clerk, and before long, they moved me up to stocking. Shortly after, my skillset revealed something unexpected, I was pretty good with flowers! I know, I'm as surprised as you! So, off I was, over into floral.

I got up to earning $6.25 an hour. It helped, but it proved to not be enough. Kevin came to Reno too, he was attending the University of Nevada while also working at Port of Subs. He would often bring home whatever sandwich fixins he could, but I still remember the one or two day bouts when I did not put a single piece of food in my mouth. I needed more money. Jill needed more money.

I needed to make a play.

I've always liked shoes, especially Jordans. I tracked down one of the largest retailers in the business, we'll call them "Kicks," an athletic shoe and apparel shop you can find in a lot of malls.

With nothing to lose, I went in there one afternoon. I sold myself, my skills, and I presented myself well, allowing my passion for their product to come through as well as the leaps I'd made in the grocery store.

They offered me a part-time gig that would net me 25 cents more per hour than the grocery store would pay me. But, to keep the job, they said I'd have to make "equal or higher sales" as the full-time employees.

It was like they either didn't want me to succeed or were trying to see how far they could push me. I wasn't sure. But I accepted, figuring I'd just learn what I needed to in real-time and get the job done.

I convinced my high school to let me out at lunch every day so I could commute and get back to work to pay my bills. I worked my tail off at Kicks, slinging Nikes, Reeboks, and Adidas. Shoes, shirts, headbands. I hustled, but was still not quite making the numbers.

Finally, one evening, I was called into the manager's office, "I have to get rid of you," he said. No warm-up, no preamble, no hesitation. I was dumbstruck.

"What can I do to stay?" I asked.

He told me that, if they can even consider keeping me, I will have to get to a full-time quota - and stay there - this week. What this represented was unreasonable and unfair standards that no one else in the company was required to do, based on the hours I worked.

But I needed to save my job. I needed to turn adversity into motivation.

I left the meeting, and, breathing slowly and deeply, I took a moment to gather my thoughts and think up anything I can do. I looked over at Jason, the Assistant Store Manager. He was part of my crew, he had my back. Jason had been there for me, he showed me the ropes. In addition, he had been giving me his own sales whenever possible to try and save my job. I would always love and respect him for that, but it was not enough. I'd need even more to save my job.

I looked out across the floor. I see the display sets of cleaners and protectants, the ones for your shoes. They sell for over ten dollars a can and I reason that they cannot take more than about twenty cents to make, but they really are a good product, and really do help your kicks stay clean.

Corporate's been pushing them, but people just haven't been keen on spending the extra dough after paying a hundred and fifty dollars for a pair of shoes. I looked out to that stack of cleaners and protectants and knew they were the only way I was saving my job. I had to do something different.

I grabbed a backpack off the shelf and filled it with bottles and samples. I took this bag and start walking around the mall observing people, their body language, their tone, and their vibe. Most importantly, I worked out how best to connect with them. I put all those psychology lessons from Dad and from my life to work, looking for all the cues for the ideal customer.

The 4 Cues to Look for in Potential Customers:

1. Look for someone approachable. This means finding someone with open body language (no crossed arms but a positive demeanor; not too involved in something else). As you receive better training, you can search for "micro-expressions" to read if someone is having a good day or bad day, if they are stressed or overwhelmed, and if they are open or shut off.
2. Look for someone who aligns with the product you are attempting to sell. My product was geared towards a younger audience who liked shoes; someone who would be willing to pay over a hundred dollars for Jordans would be willing to buy something to protect them.
3. Look for someone you feel you could relate to or be friends with, or even someone you could see yourself just having a conversation with. Starting with you being comfortable is key—then, as you get more comfortable, there won't be anyone you are not willing to approach.
4. Look for the right situation. If you approach someone to buy shoe cleaner while they are juggling bags or buying their kids ice cream from the food court, you'll probably get a "no." But if you approach a kid wandering the store with his girlfriend and you roll up and compliment them, make them feel like the "cool kid" for their shoes, it's often an easy "yes."

4 Things to Avoid: What to NEVER do to make a sale:

1. Never force someone to talk to you. Be friendly and positive and start as if you are trying to make a friend, not make a sale.
2. Never sell to someone that doesn't need your product. In this example, I'm looking for a kid with Jordans, not a middle-aged woman in high heels.
3. Never speak over the potential customer. If they start to talk, you stop talking and listen. Use their verbal cues as a way to begin guiding your sales pitch to the next level.
4. Never force the close, but always ask for the sale. Many people fail to just simply ask the person to buy their product. Don't force someone to buy your product, and don't push past a person's patience, but it never hurts to kindly ask if someone wants to hear about and buy your product.

Back to me at the mall slinging shoe protectant to save my job:

"Hey, you gotta check this out," I'd say when I spotted someone my instincts told me would work, "Let me show you my stuff!"

I sold the cleaners and protectants right out of my backpack, walking up and down the mall for a couple of hours. I sold forty. The store hadn't sold that many in four months!

Happy with my work, I headed back into the store and eagerly told my boss what I had just done. He did not seem too thrilled, this was not the conventional way of selling, nor was it strictly within policy, but he couldn't turn a blind eye to the revenue. Through this, I kept my job, at least for a while longer. And I kept selling products out of a bag for a few hours a day.

Several days later, the Vice President of the company called me out of the blue and, after a short conversation, he said, "Hey, keep doing what you are doing. We are noticing."

I'll never forget that call—getting noticed. Getting noticed for doing something good. At the time, recognition was my form of success. A light switch went off in my head: *Sales—this was my gig.*

It's worth noting that, for many, recognition is more important than success. I've worked with many people like this throughout the years. Even in sales, where money is a driver, some simply want to be recognized by people for doing a good job. They want the pedestal, and the "well dones." If you are struggling to motivate a team member, try praise and recognition. It may just be their driver.

I'm a fan of team meetings, not the long, drawn-out, endless, pointless discussions day after day, but the important ones. The ones I would hold weekly for recognition. My "weekly round-up" would consist of a quick overview of major projects, then would morph into public praise toward those deserving recognition. This was huge for the team to gain recognition from leadership in front of the entire team. We could use words, sometimes certificates, or even a simple Starbucks gift card to get a round of applause for the person receiving it. For success, never use this as a time to punish, this will create the opposite effect. I suggest doing that in private and using public forums for praise only.

There is a deep impact for receiving hype up in front of others. Outside of these, when production was slowing, I would mix it up and walk around handing out praise. The days where'd I get the highest productivity were the days when I did this. We all deserve to receive praise and thanks for the efforts we put in daily.

A few weeks later, this success transferred to my sneaker sales, and I became the top-selling member of the team. My new candor and attitude with customers mean that my conversion rate soared to new peaks.

As a result, I received another call. This time, I'm told that there's a Kicks location nearby and they want me to take over as an Assistant Manager.

I'm thrilled; it's a two dollar raise and it's outside of a mall, which was starting to wear on me a bit. I head over and meet the manager, Connor. Connor had heard about me from my colleagues and the Regional Manager; I had started to develop a bit of a reputation. He wanted to grow his numbers and respected what he had heard about my work ethic. Plus, he was into anime too. We bonded right away, and it seemed like I'd found a bright future.

I came into work the next day for my first day as Assistant Manager, and he asked me to open up the store while he went back into his office and made some phone calls.

I opened up, not really sure what to do, and I expected him to come out relatively soon to show me the ropes. However, he remained in his office for hours on the phone. I was doing what I could to run the store without him, and I made some mistakes alongside some sales, but overall it went fairly well.

Then, at the end of the day, Connor finally came out of his office. Immediately, I knew something was up; I could see it in his body language.

"Sorry kid," he said, dolefully, "they just transferred me to Idaho. The store is yours."

I was a little shocked and, despite my trepidation, I was pretty stoked. He gave me the keys and was gone. I didn't even have the login or passwords to the computer.

I quickly realized that I needed some help. I would have turned to Jason, but he had recently left the company, so I was on my own. One thing I knew, even at the age of 17, was to recognize my own limitations. I could start winging it, and I may have gotten it right, but if I didn't it would be me that was held accountable, so I looked for some help.

I started going down the list and calling other Kicks locations for assistance. The first couple did not get me anywhere, but then I called a store in Tahoe, and not only did the guy pick up, but he also actually listened to me.

"Wow, that's messed up," he said, his incredulity clear over the phone, "let me see how I can help you."

He did, and after our call, I can finally log in to the network.

He couldn't help me with my new team though. I gathered them up and told them about Connor being transferred to Idaho.

"So… I'm your boss now," I told them. This, upon reflection, was an error. I think about how I would have reacted in that situation, if I had worked in this store for any period of time, and then one day, this new kid comes in and is suddenly in charge. Maybe I too would have felt aggrieved. I should have softened this message a bit and added some empathy.

As I finished telling them the situation, almost immediately, like some staged performance, everybody took off their uniforms and walked out of the store. They weren't going to answer to some kid.

I didn't know what to do with myself. Five minutes ago, I had a store with a full team. Now, it's just me, in this empty store, not equipped to deal with any of this, just standing there alone. Vulnerable.

I had a moment of panic. My head began turning from one thought to the next: I have bills to pay, and I have Jill to care for. I don't know what to do.

After several minutes of reconciliation, I turned to someone I knew I could rely on. I called Kevin. Kevin is my guy. Kevin will help.

I called him up and convinced him to quit his job at Port of Subs and come work for me at Kicks.

"Fine," he reluctantly said, "but don't be expecting me to call you 'boss' or anything."

I learned a lot in my early career, and Kicks unwittingly taught me a ton. As Connor walked out, followed quickly by his old team, I learned the value of networking and building alliances.

My first instinct was to turn to those who I believed could help. Because I was so new to this community of managers, I did not know anybody, so it took a dozen or so calls to finally get to someone willing to help. Of those that answered before Tahoe, they had no motivation to help. It was late in the day; their only motivation was to get home.

If they knew me, had a personal relationship, or even had an awareness of me, this may have been different. I vowed to never let this happen, so now, I have built, and encourage others to build their own alliances and networks. This book is even a part of that process!

After Tahoe defied expectations and helped me, they became a part of my network. Naturally, I turned to my key ally and the center of my network. When I turned to Kevin, Kevin did not disappoint, and it is my relationship with Kevin that reminds me daily about the importance of building strong relationships.

Over the next few months, with Kevin's help, I rebuilt the store. We began to outperform every store in my area, and even though we did not have the walk-up business as the mall stores did, we were moving products.

How did I do it? I never said "no." When a store had a customer looking for the Jordan XI in a men's size twelve and didn't have it, they called around to see if someone else does. A lot of stores would answer these calls with an instinct to just say ""no"; they didn't want to bother looking around for one and holding it for a customer who may never come.

But when a store called me, I would always say "yes." No matter what. Even if I knew I didn't have those Jordan XIs in a size twelve, I'd say I did (I know, sounds awful, but I was trying everything I could). This practice of always saying "yes" at least got people inside the store, because, whether we had the shoes or not, I knew I could help them out and get them to leave the store with something.

Things went well for a while. Our store became kind of like this little hangout, this little haven for "Sneaker Heads." I knew this world—knew sports and how people who liked sports preferred to dress. And I could sell to other young people well. I learned a lot about how to talk to people from Steve and Mike. I started to approach customers and begin talking with them, pumping them up, pumping up our products. Our numbers grew, and I started to get comfortable with all the new realms of my job.

Pay attention to the person's body language and voice. If it's open and non-aggressive, ask again, this time in a new and different way. This often works. If it doesn't, the person is probably just trying to be polite but is not interested, so stop and wish them a good day. Never push too hard.

Also, in sales, if you get a "no," it often means "I'm unsure." This is a 'soft no,' and I encourage following up by asking what the objection is or giving another reason they should buy.

I realize this might sound like a basic tip, but I am amazed at how often I teach this. So for those that know it, this is a reminder. If you don't use this rule, I highly recommend you apply it to your process.

Running your own store as a kid isn't easy; at least, it wasn't for me, but I started to make a lot more money which meant I could take better care of Jill.

And, before I could vote, I'd put a down payment on a house. For us. For Jill and me.

I graduated high school in June, bought the house in July. By September, Jill and I were married.

HONEYMOON

I was working non-stop, and Kicks had become my life. I took about an hour's commute to work each day, and each day, I had to arrive an hour early so Jill had time to get to work. This meant that I was mostly working alone as Kevin was in college most of the day. I would regularly run inventory alone, before, *and* after we close. I did not get breaks, no days off—I had little to zero support, and I was burning out.

But I was number one in the territory.

I was also just about to get married, and Jill and I wanted to organize our honeymoon. We wanted to do it right, to celebrate it right. Having never been on a vacation in my life (when I was a child, we were too poor to go camping), I called to tell the Regional that I had vacation time that I wanted to use.

"I'll give you one day off for your wedding. But that's it," his booming voice told me.

Well damn, I thought, and I figure that's the end of that. Jill then showed up at work, knowing that I was going to be calling to request leave that day, and she was so excited about our trip. I stuttered and stumbled my way through an explanation that, no, we wouldn't be able to go. Her face dropped, and her shoulders drooped. Seeing her disappointment extended my frustration. I was overwhelmed by the knowledge that I was working so hard, yet this was not the life I promised her.

Then the frustration turned to anger, and I lost it. I lost all rationality and control, desperate to show Jill that she came first, not work. I went over to the phone in the front of the store and started calling every store in the territory.

"Hi, this is Billy Thompson from store dot-dot-dot, and you can go f*** yourself."

I hung up and called the next store, telling them that they too can go f*** themselves. I made it all the way to the end of the list, to the VP. I called him too, and told him: "You run a sh***y company, and you can go f*** yourself."

So, yeah, it ruffled some feathers. I for sure thought me and Kicks were done. A nice little run and now onto the next hustle.

After my little tirade, it sort of came out that none of the higher-ups knew I was really running the store on my own. They probably got nervous about that. I do know that the VP called the Regional, who was vacationing in Hawaii. Yeah, he called him right up and they had a conversation, and he made the guy fly home early to come and watch my store—made him watch the store for one full week *before* my wedding and then two full weeks *after*. I don't know if they were just trying to not get sued or what, but they gave me the P.T.O., bumped my pay, *and* gave me a bonus.

It felt great, getting to go on a genuine honeymoon to celebrate our vows, properly. It was a giant island that made that sea of bad like a distant pond.

When the vacation was up and Jill and I got home, I wasn't sure what to do about Kicks. It felt like the path was over, but I was still walking it. I was "successful," far beyond what the company expected from me. Far beyond what anyone should expect from a kid barely making his way out of high school. I was number one in the territory: lowest shrinkage, highest conversion rates— and already being asked to relocate to other problem stores to replicate what I did in Nevada. It was a success, sure, just not MY SUCCESS. The way I was working and the way I was being treated, it was taking away from what was important to me: time with my Jill.

Then, out of the clear blue sky one day, I received an offer on a gig to run a cell phone store. With a strong opportunity to make a change to find MY SUCCESS, I dove in headfirst.

I understand the details of the job—to sell cell phones at a little mom-and-pop (electronics and printing) shop. It had minimal commission with lower pay, so I was going to take a huge hit financially. *But maybe I'll have some sanity*, I think. So, I quit Kicks and start working for Connect slinging cell phones. It's a small business with not many employees but it gives me a lot of agency.

First, I got to do a re-lay of the store, placing the products according to how my instincts told me to. I knew, like anyone else, that if you get the customer to pick something up, even just get them to look at something, that gets the ball rolling. I studied every day, observing people's reactions when they walked into the store. It was different from Kicks. With cell phones, I was selling a contract with an expensive device, so the sale took much longer. Repeat traffic was minimal except for accessories, so I was learning to develop a deeper bond for each sale.

I learned daily; honed my craft. I was there for four years as I continued my education in sales. I was pretty motivated, and I wanted to blow their records out of the water. I was all about, "let's go make more money."

Moving from Kicks to Connect was me walking away from what most would call "success," to pursue my own version of success. I was home more with Jill. We got to see each other more; I had far less pressure and stress. I was moving in the right direction.

Sure, the pay was less but I was happily working hard while still being able to have more time with Jill.

ANIMAL CRACKERS

So, I'd quit Kicks, and Jill and I were struggling financially. One day always sticks out in my mind. On this day, we were walking the aisles of the grocery store. Jill had a detailed list with prices, an envelope of coupons, and a strict budget.

I strayed from Jill and the cart and saw some animal crackers up on the shelf. They were calling my name. I love those things, especially the frosted ones… damn, they're good. I walked up and grabbed a box before walking back to Jill and the cart.

I was about to put them in and was excited to do so when she looked at me. She was nearly in tears.

"Billy," she said, "we can't afford those."

I walked back down the aisle and put the animal crackers back up on the shelf. Right before I put them down, I looked down at the price tag to see how much they cost.

They were a dollar.

One dollar.

One hundred measly not-even-pure-copper-anymore pennies.

I vowed never to have this happen again.

I wasn't upset with my wife. I wasn't upset at the world, and I wasn't upset at the animal crackers. I was upset with myself.

So, I made a change.

Instead of just chasing money, I started chasing ideas. I started to chase my own concepts and interpretations rather than "what the messaging was telling me."

If a single dollar was throwing off our entire budget, something had to change. I was working too hard, and though I don't know if you like animal crackers or not, I bet, at some point in your life - if not *right now* - you are working too hard, and I bet you are doing it for not enough.

We have to challenge ourselves to trust what our inner voice is telling us so that we may go beyond the rigged game and start living our "unique-to-you" success: what it looks and feels like; because that is where we *should* live. Generational cycles do exist - and in tons of different ways - but they do not need to define us. In fact, they must not. And those generational cycles, at their core, are just the stories we tell about ourselves. When we change our story, we sure as heck can change its ending.

Now I've got to ask you—what does your "go beyond" look like? Will you stop following the lie? How will you break the rigged game to find YOUR SUCCESS?

When pursuing YOUR SUCCESS, it can get frustrating. Not being able to afford a simple pack of cookies can make you want to give up. I get it, but this is where it is vital to understand where you are heading to remain positive. Throughout the book, you'll continue to see how my attitude and determination

drove MY SUCCESS, and it can for you as well. You must believe that you can be successful, remain positive on the approach, and work toward that success and you will find YOUR SUCCESS. Our minds are a powerful thing, it is proven in psychology that even faking a smile can positively impact your mood. Triggering muscles to force a smile tricks your brain into thinking you are happy.

When you force a smile, even if it isn't real, your brain starts to release tiny molecules called neuropeptides, as well as other neurotransmitters including endorphins, serotonin, and dopamine. These can help fight stress, work as a pain reliever, and act as an antidepressant. Taking the conscious effort to force a smile in the hard times can act as a tool to support you through the moment. Remain positive, as long as you don't give up, you can make it through.

Our struggle changed when the market went crazy in '06, we sold our house and made a boatload of money. After we closed, I logged in and took a look at our bank account. "Screw it," I said to Jill, "let's take a year off of work."

A big smile spread across her face, and so we did. We took a year off and just get to know each other. We traveled the West Coast and made it down to Arizona to reconnect with my mom and little sister, Samantha. They were back living in Yuma, Samantha was now three and Mom was able to escape her generational cycle to find success for her and her daughter.

We bounced around looking for new adventures. Most importantly, we spent endless amounts of time together. Then, one day, I had this idea, something like: "I hate time… so let's just go without time for a week."

Jill was game. We removed all watches and clocks and knowledge of time from our lives and just flowed. It was an amazing experience to just let life be. Removing time taught us that life isn't controlled by a hand on a clock but rather managed by the process of how we *spend* our time.

When we removed time, we ate when we were hungry, and slept when we were tired. A few days in, we reached points where we'd be waking up and not sure if the sun was just going down or just coming up. We flowed. When we choose to do something, we'd consider what we wanted to do, rather than how long we had to do it.

The whole year of no work was our year of bliss. We took one whole year off from the grind to just know each other. We took time to get to know ourselves and find what made us happy. If I wanted to watch an entire anime series, it didn't matter that it was twenty hours long, it was just something I wanted to do. If my wife wanted to read an entire book, she didn't have to stop because she had to go to bed to be able to wake up early for work the next morning. We embraced life and spent our time on the things we wanted to do and not on what the world taught us to do with it.

We discovered that there was something more valuable than diamonds, gold, or money. We discovered the value of Time.

Time is an asset - *the* asset, really - the most valuable thing on the planet, but one that most people spend without truly acknowledging. We too often give it away too easily. But, because of the deaths I've endured in my life, I can tell you that there is never enough Time.

So, as you continue reading and discovering what YOUR SUCCESS looks like, I encourage you to understand that Time is the most important asset.

Part Four

"As you live you lose reasons and hope. But as you keep on going, you pick up new reasons and hope."

- Asta Staria, Black Clover

LOSING JILL

I was finding the sea of calm in my life—a rare phenomenon. Returning from a year off with my Jill deepened our relationship, established an unbreakable friendship, and prepared us for the happily ever after we both dreamed of.

But my life has never been that simple.

After a year in paradise, I found it hard to come back to the grind. After getting back home and starting up work again, I was motivated to build our future, but at the same time, I was content with what we had.

We had reached a good place and made enough to take a year off and begin building a new house for our future. It was a calm sea.

Then it all changed.

Late one night, I was woken up to my Jill's screaming voice. The pain I heard in her broke my heart. Something was wrong with her stomach, but I did not know what to do. She told me that she's got terrible cramps and just needed to make it through. I followed her directions and gathered meds and a heat pack to help. But that night was one of the longest, most agonizing times of my life. I begged to take her to the hospital, but she refused. We didn't have the insurance or the money. I was once again feeling like a failure.

Finally, after the all-night run of pain, I convinced her to go in.

Like most in our situation with no insurance, we were treated as such. Put to the side, ignored, leading me to pace the halls of the ER, yelling at any doctor I see. Hours begin to pass; the doctors argued that her blood work was normal as they hinted that they would not give her any pain pills. I could tell they expected us to be poor and hungry for a high. We argued that something was wrong and that we did not want pain pills. They made us wait even more.

Finally, after hours of waiting, they ordered a CT of her belly.

The rest still feels like a blur. Moments after the scan, they came out rushing around, put her on a bed, hooked her up to monitors, and got an IV ready; everyone was panicking.

"Your appendix has ruptured. If we don't operate immediately, you'll die." I freeze. I just cannot lose Jill.

I saw the same fear in my Jill's eyes, and tears fell freely down our faces. I looked up, reading the doctor's body language and micro-expressions leading me to the conclusion that this is bad, really bad. His eyes told me that I needed to say goodbye. I refused.

"Come back to me, my love," I told her gently, with a kiss on her forehead.

As she was taken back beyond the point I can follow, I felt my soul fall out of my body. In my life, this had become normal, yet it was never a surprise and was always painful. I could feel that the love of my life, the one person that made me feel like I am not alone, my best friend, my lover, my soul mate, may have just spoken to me for the last time.

I was left in a waiting room, alone once again. I was sick from emotion, I was hurting, and I needed to leave. I rushed out of the room, down the hall, and stumbled on a door leading to a stairwell. I went in.

I was angry, and the world had once again tossed me out to sea with no life raft. I was awash with the emotions of losing Mike, and losing my father, blended with a life of trauma; they all came rushing back in.

"I'm going to be alone again? I can't…" I said aloud in the hospital stairwell I had found myself hiding in.

"I can't do this anymore." The feelings of quitting life were filling my soul. I could feel the pain start to dissipate as I went numb.

All I could think was, *what about our happily ever after? What about finally having something good in my life? What about me not being alone anymore. God, this is more than I can bear, so why? I'm done! I can't anymore. No more of this. DO YOU HEAR ME? I'M DONE!*

As my thoughts wandered into the darkness, I felt a hand on my shoulder, bringing my vision back to the world around me.

"You're the husband, right?" The deep voice belonged to a man nearly twice my size, muscular, and rough with a biker vibe, dressed in blue scrubs.

"Yeah..." I barely got the words out as tears fell heavily down my cheek.

"You're so young…" He said quietly, almost to himself, as if surprised to be first meeting me, "I was just in there with her, you know" he explained.

This surprised me, as I had yet to tell anyone where I was hiding, entirely away from the waiting room in case I was about to do something stupid.

"I stayed to make sure, so don't worry," he continued.

"Make sure? Make sure of what?" I asked.

"I stayed until I knew she was going to be ok. She IS going to be ok." This man, this complete stranger, but someone who had given me the best news I had heard in my short life, wrapped me up in a bear hug, one of the most kind, genuine hugs I'd ever felt.

"They'll be out soon to tell you such, so get back in there, she's going to need you. Promise me you'll stay by her side, ok?"

"Always."

He patted me on the back with a hard shove to get my feet in motion. Halfway down the hall, I looked back at the man. He was still standing there as if waiting to ensure I make it safely to the room I had left. He waved with a smile as I walked back into the surgery waiting room.

As predicted, moments later I am told the surgery was rough, but they successfully saved my Jill's life. I asked about the nurse that came to speak with me, and no one knew who I was talking about.

He may have been an observer, overhead the situation, or something else. Either way, whatever it was, it kept me around to protect my Jill, and I'm thankful for that.

NEW APPROACH

The following couple of months were rough. Jill was trying to recover, but the surgery took its toll. She was bedridden for a while, the scar ran up her entire belly, and she was so weak that she had to learn to walk again. I would be by her side through it all.

I began to research physical therapy at night while she slept so that the next morning, I could be her coach. I would motivate her, work with her, and apply all my baseball training and coaching lessons to help her get better fast. The nurses and physical therapists quickly learned that she responded to me like no one else, so they'd give me the objectives and let me take over. I spent every moment with her; nothing could pull me away from her side.

We were going to get our happily ever after, and nothing would stop that from happening.

But as I've mentioned, my life isn't that simple.

After recovery, the time she missed at work resulted in her being fired. Crazy right? You're hospitalized, almost died, and come back to learn you no longer have a job. This is painful for many reasons and can be summarized according to three heartaches:

ONE: She felt betrayed by her company. Working hard meant nothing, she was just another number, and they moved on without hesitation.

TWO: We'd just finished building our house, and we needed both incomes to support this purchase.

THREE: Without insurance, our medical debt was astronomical.

I needed to do more. I needed to fix this for her and our future. I didn't care what it would take, I got my Jill back, and I was now ready to work even harder.

Part of our appreciation for our new life led us to decide to have a child. For us, life was short. We knew this fact. Why wait? Sure, we were in debt and struggling, but we wanted to start a family.

Finding out Jill was pregnant was one of the happiest moments of my life. I knew I wanted to have a child; I knew I wanted to have a "normal" life. I knew I wanted Jill to have the picture-perfect world I'd seen in TV sitcoms growing up. A place of love, connection, and family.

Jill aligned the finances, we got payment plans in place, and we were going to make it work; our own version of happily ever after.

I started working harder with Connect, finding new ways to reach audiences. If I applied a moment of personal connection to each person, I could relate, identify needs, and make the sale. I needed to evolve to make more money, to provide for my family. I found there was a series of habits that, if followed, would attract customers my way and drive my numbers up.

I begin to build a new process.

The Four Ps to Your Sales Process:
Preparation, Presence, Passion, Pliable.

Preparation – How can you sell a product when you don't know about the product? Before I sell a product or allow a salesperson to sell, I ensure the product is known inside and out. You must study the product, all aspects, know the pricing, know the particulars, and know what you expect the client to gain from purchasing this product. You must prepare for your sales, which will build confidence in your customer, which comes from the knowledge that you are the expert in what they are considering purchasing.

Presence – During sales, my body language is always open, I am attentive, and when a customer approaches me, they know that they have my full attention. I invite them to use my time so we can reach the sale they are looking for. My demeanor is open and ready for the client to approach me.

Passion– Someone is about to spend money with you. Shouldn't you feel good and excited about it if you are about to give up something that took your time to earn? With each customer I face, I give the respect and positive approach they deserve for the money they are about to give. Then, I add a bit of enthusiasm and make the sales process enjoyable. I make the client feel good about their purchases by reassuring them of their decision, complimenting them, and giving time to each client as if they are my only client. Your approach toward selling a product should have passion and drive. This will come through in your sales process. If the customer feels good about the purchase, not only do you avoid returns, but you also assure a repeat in business for their subsequent purchases.

Pliable – The sales process is unique and requires one to be adaptable. Regardless of the product, during the closing conversation, new barriers arise, situations occur, and you have to be able to think on your feet. This requires preparation (as noted above) and being flexible to the client's needs in the conversation rather than how you want the process to go.

Applying these steps kicked my store sales up significantly. I was making a bit more money, starting to pay down debt, and things were looking up. Then, as my life goes, the weather shifted, and the seas changed.

FINDING A NEW PATH

The pregnancy was normal by our comparable standards. We enjoyed the process, the time together, and the late-night Jack-in-the-Box taco runs Jill would send me on. We grew even closer, getting ready to welcome Keiren into the world.

As we passed her due date, an induction was scheduled. Everything continued to be normal right up to Jill's water breaking. At that moment, Keiren's heartbeat began to drop rapidly. Something was wrong. Like the last time, I read the doctor. It was bad. Jill was rushed to surgery once more.

We didn't know at the time, but the previous surgery resulted in major internal issues for Jill, including limited space from scar tissue for Keiren to grow. As this occurred, the umbilical cord was wrapped around her throat multiple times. When the water broke, she began to be strangled. My daughter was dying.

Once more, I had to say goodbye to my love quickly and pray she would return to me.

"Come back to me, my love," I told her again. But this time, I wouldn't lose hope. This time I would have faith. This time I would be ready to take care of my girls when they came back to me.

My daughter came out first after a dangerous "crash" C-section. Keiren Thompson, Ren, was born, and my life changed. I held this miracle in my hands, knowing I would never be the same. Keiren, or Ren, shouldn't have been able to survive this, but the doctors told me this amazing child held her tiny hands on the cord, preventing complete suffocation. Ren wanted to live, so I would be there for her, always and no matter what.

I was able to bathe my daughter, bond with her, and get to know her while we both waited for her mother. I was a father but couldn't embrace pure joy as my Jill was still in surgery. I held my baby, full of pride, excited, and in love, yet my wife was not with me, and I was heartbroken and worried about her.

It would be hours before she was wheeled back. Jill almost died again. The love of my life was almost gone. Yet, somehow, both my girls made it back to me. At this moment, I knew I would need to be more for them.

With this new surgery, our debt grew fiercely. On top of that, it was now 2008 and the recession was in full swing. We were not only in medical debt, we were now upside down in our mortgage. Our finite credit was shrinking.

I was going in the wrong direction. I didn't just have no money; I owed an unattainable amount. At my current pay rate, we would never pay off the debt, never break even, and never have the life I wanted for my family. I needed to do something big.

I realized this debt would not be resolved in our lifetime at my current pace. I needed to go bigger than Connect. I was already learning how valuable time was, but I didn't have a choice anymore. I needed a way to pay for this debt. I needed to build a better life for my family. I wasn't going to allow Jill and my child to face poverty. I lived that life. It wasn't enough, and my girls deserved more.

I needed to go bigger—and I guess maybe I was putting out that vibe because one day, this guy in a business suit with perfectly combed hair entered the store, and I started chumming it up with him. Taking my approach, I bonded with him and sold him a new phone. Then I sold him a new phone for his wife. And then a new phone for his kid. A few more things too.

By the time he was heading out the door, the guy was holding a full bag in each arm.

He stopped at the door, turned back around, looked at me, and said, "You know, I came in here just to pick up one single charger."

"I am so sorry." I said fearfully. I knew my sale was on point, and maybe even a bit over the top .

He quickly reassured me that he was not mad.

"Do you think," he said, indicating his overflowing bags of phones, cords, and accessories, "that you could do this for beds?"

"I can sell anything."

Little did I know, he was not selling mattresses. He was filling beds—in a skilled nursing facility. The curriculum was about to get a lot tougher.

Part Five

"A-B-C, A-Always, B-Be, C-Closing, Always Be Closing."

- Blake, Glengarry Glen Ross

SELLING BEDS

The job was for Director of Marketing and Sales for a skilled nursing company that we will call The Estates. They were well established out in Illinois with sixty or so sites and had just reached Nevada after looking to expand.

I went through the interview process, and things went well.

The Executive Director, James (the same man I sold all those cell phones to), told me that he thinks I can do this, and passed me up the ladder. I got on the phone with the Regional, Misty, and she said: "Well, I don't know why I'm interviewing a kid for this, but…"

Turns out, she thought she would get fired if she hired me; thought everyone would think her an idiot for hiring a kid.

But she was intrigued by me, I could tell. I needed to make a play. I needed to take care of my family.

"I'll do it for less than you'd pay someone else," I said.

Misty hired me on the spot. "But," she said, "I'm going to hold you accountable to the job, not to your age." In doing so, she gave me my first real opportunity for a career, something I'll always appreciate and love her for.

"Okay, let's do this," I told her.

Fast forward to my first week on the job: I got a company car and I was off to talk to doctors. That was the job, to try and get them to send their seniors our way. The business was based on the referral. These referrals came from doctor's offices, senior living communities, medical facilities, and hospitals.

You have to build relationships, prove your product is safe, and convince them to send people to you instead of your competitors.

The job didn't have a commission but offered a much higher salary. I needed it – Jill and Ren needed it – and I needed to earn my keep. In the first week, I was hired to fill the building with skilled nursing. Step one was to go to each doctor's office in my area and schedule a lunch meeting of sorts with them so I could convince them to send their patients our way.

Just a couple of days in, I went to my first doctor's office. I walked in and before I even finished my pitch, the lady behind the counter yelled, "If you don't get out, I'm going to call the police!"

I backed out: "I'm sorry. I don't know what I did."

It was not exactly the type of reception I was prepared for. I left the office and called my boss.

"Oh yeah, that's normal," he told me, nonchalantly, "We had a situation with one of their patients that ended in some bad press. It's normal."

"What?" I said, exasperated.

"We've got a bad reputation. Your job is to go out and fix it."

I'm in trouble, I told myself. Ren had only recently come into the world, and I had just spent two hundred bucks on a jacket and tie—I couldn't have this thing not work out. I went back to those childhood lessons, back to Dad and me just driving around and selling baked goods door-to-door.

I drove down the street and found a Starbucks; I got a bunch of flavored coffees and little pastries, and I put them on a tray and returned to the same office that just kicked me out. *I just have to connect to them,* I told myself, *connect to people. This is my job.*

I went back to the office and opened the door, deciding to use psychology to prove that I wasn't a threat. I got down, as low as I could, chest almost to the floor, and I started crawling to the front desk, saying (pleading really), "Please don't arrest me, please don't arrest me." I had the tray in one hand and a napkin in my other hand in place of a white flag, making a big to-do out of it.

"Can I stand up without you calling the police?" I asked. My approach showed that I meant no harm, that I was humble enough to crawl and beg for forgiveness. The result was a positive response.

"Yes, yes, just get up."

I decided to continue this openness. I just laid it all out, completely vulnerable.

"This is my first day on the job. My wife just had a baby. If I don't have a meeting by the end of the day, it's not going to be good. I'm sorry. I don't know what I did wrong. I just want to talk with you." *With* is key here. *With* implies conversation, not a sales pitch. I am not talking *to* them.

The nurses came toward me. They told me they were sorry for how they acted; they blamed it on everything that had gone on before.

"I'm here to make sure you don't have those situations," I said as I smiled and handed them some coffee and pastries.

They took me into the back room and brought out the doctor, agreeing to hear me out. I went to work, and we all ate pastries and drank coffee together. I connected with them, as human beings, and together, we began to fix that bad situation and drive success.

That was my first week.

I live in rural Nevada. Other than Reno, there is no city, and you can go for long stretches without seeing much other than sagebrush and wild horses. A lot of these doctor's offices are two or three hours away.

I was driving to Hawthorne one day when a rockslide came down off the cliff and slammed into the car, denting the bumper and nearly caving in the roof.

I couldn't believe it. Of all the luck or complete lack thereof. All of my thoughts were negative. All I kept thinking about was the mountain crashing down into me. I had finally gotten a solid chance at making some money and now, I would probably owe on the car.

It would have been easy for me to spiral into my misery, but once again, I switched my mindset. Switched my thinking. I cleared away some of the debris and trudged on. The car somehow made it the last few miles down the highway, and I relaxed and went into my meeting confident.

I told the doc what happened, about the rockslide, and how I don't have a way home. I walked him outside and showed him the wreckage. He saw that I wasn't fooling him.

"You wanna go have lunch?" I asked.

We went to lunch, and by relaxing and using the stressful situation as an "in" to start the conversation, I was able to create a bond with this doctor. Typically, the doctor would have said "no," and I would have been lucky to land a meeting within three to four months, but here we were, sitting at lunch and enjoying a conversation.

That's why I say that life is about connections—about bonds. After that rockslide, I could have given up, turned back around, and let it ruin my day. Instead, rather than soak in self-pity, I used it to generate a conversation that sparked multiple closed deals.

I again relied on psychology, and how the science/art is not just the study of the mind and behavior in *others*, but also key to understanding OUR mind and OUR behavior. It's not just about being a "glass half full" person either. It's about understanding that *life happens*, and so it is all about how we respond, and how we move forward. None of us can go back in time and change something about our lives. But we can all, from right now onwards, go and do the things that help us improve our futures.

In sales, we sometimes forget that we are selling to people. We forget that people have feelings, likes, dislikes, and even compassion. A single conversation steeped in vulnerability can connect you with others. For me, it was a crashed car and switching from a negative take to a positive approach that, at the core, is what closed that deal. For you, it could be opening up about spilling your coffee on your new suit or waking up late, or anything else that is somewhat self-deprecating that others can relate to.

A couple of weeks later, Misty came out and said, "Patrick, I know you're new at this, but you need to write a marketing plan for your building."

Patrick. That's my given name. Patrick William Thompson III. To this day, Misty is the only person who's ever really called me by that name.

"A marketing plan?" I asked. I did not know how to write a marketing plan. I had not been to college, and I did not even really know what a marketing plan was.

After the meeting, I went online, and started researching. I could not do what everyone else had the time to learn in college, so I planned to just work harder.

Equipped with the attitude that I would take all my free time and teach myself, I would learn what the heck a marketing plan truly was and go from there.

I read on, making connections to what I had been doing all along, all the way back to selling those cookies with my dad. I put names to concepts and reverse-engineered how I should attack this marketing plan. I put it together and outlined my entire vision. It had a series of bullet points that described what needed to be achieved and how to accomplish it.

Most marketing plans give the premise of what needs to be done, but I took the time to outline, then in detail describe exactly how I was going to accomplish this.

I put this thing together and the next day the higher-ups came out and I outlined my vision. To my immense relief, it went over pretty darn well. They were excited; they even asked to take a copy and share it with the home office.

I was proud of myself for working hard, creating the plan, and getting some great feedback on it. Despite my tough first week, I started crushing it. It did not take long before I was moving people into the facility at a record pace. But, more so than records for this position, the success was in fixing the bad publicity the business had within the community. This location was thought to have been a lost cause, a problem building, somewhere you'd never refer to. I turned it around into being the number one choice to refer clients to in all markets—primary, secondary, and tertiary.

GOING EXECUTIVE

Fast forward three months.

My phone rang. It was the owner of the company, Don, and he told me how they wanted me to come out to a conference. They usually only took longtime employees and directors and such to these things, but Don wanted me to be there in person. He had plans for me.

Don was a big dog, and not just in the industry. This was a man of power. We're friends now, but back then I was simply in awe. He was powerful, wealthy, and yet would roll into one of his buildings super casual-like, in jeans and flannel button-ups. He built this phenomenal company from nothing, simply for his mom. At the time, Illinois didn't have the proper care facilities, so when his mom needed care, he built it and has run each property as if his own mother was living in it ever since.

I respected that greatly. Still do.

I met up with my new Executive Director. By this point, James was already gone (the position felt like the *Defense Against the Dark Arts* post at *Hogwarts*—no one stuck around too long).

I already missed him; he is, to this day, someone I greatly respect and with whom I'll continue to stay connected to throughout my life.

The new Executive Director and I flew out to Illinois. I met Don, Misty, and the rest of the home office team, and seemed to make a good impression with my drive and upbeat attitude.

Still, like some big sister trying to keep her little brother in check, Misty was constantly telling me, "Ok now, Patrick, calm it down." To this day, she still talks to me in the tone, but I like it—I know it's genuine and with love.

They explained to me that I was going to go visit one of the facilities.

"Okay," I said, eager to please.

In no time at all, I was shipped out to get trained up. I found myself sitting in this lady's office. She was going to be my trainer. I was eager and ready to learn, but before we really got going, I noticed a packet on her desk. It says "sales and marketing" on it. It's a really bad cover. Big colors, bad font choices.

"Is this your marketing plan?" I asked.

"No, that's the company-mandated marketing plan."

I asked if I could take a look. After turning over that awful, garish cover, I started reading. It read familiar. *Real* familiar. That's because, darn near word for word, I was looking at my own marketing plan!

"This is my marketing plan," I said.

She laughed as though I had just told her some funny joke.

"No, seriously, I wrote this months ago." I invited her over and we looked at it together. I told her the story, and we went through the plan and, by how well I know it, she admitted that maybe I should be training her. I felt pride in my efforts. Not only was I able to create something strong enough for my position, but it was catching on company wide. This proved to my young ego that my ideas were valuable, that I was worth something and capable of anything.

I didn't make a big deal about them using my plan, but when I brought it up, Misty reminded me, "Now don't go getting a big head Patrick, you've still got a lot to learn." Of course, she was right, but it felt good, and I kept trucking forward.

I spent the week training rather than being trained, but an evening full of chaos almost disrupted my progress.

At the hotel one night, I came back to the room which was shared by my new boss to find it full of people. It was nearing the end of the week and people apparently had some steam to let loose and a party had broken out. Everyone was drunk, people were doing things they should not be, and they wanted me to join in.

But I had bigger plans than an evening of fun. I had goals to reach because I knew I must find MY SUCCESS. So, I grabbed a pillow off the bed and found a quiet place in the stairwell of the hotel, and managed to grab some sleep.

Don was starting to see how different I was; how I wanted a different life. He wanted me to grow with the company, and he and Misty took me under their wing. He told me that he sees "great things" in me, and this motivated me further. I could have stayed with the company forever, but I had to go back to Nevada. It was only our separate physical location that kept me from the success I could have found with Don and Misty.

Thing is, the rotating door into the Executive Director's office kept rotating.

"Patrick," Don told me one day after another one had just left, "I need you to handle things until we get a new director in place. You can handle that right?"

"Sure thing," I replied, a phrase I'd started to use, always saying yes, always taking the challenge.

Over the next few months, I supported the facility as a Marketing Director while also taking on random responsibilities that would typically fall to the Executive Director. I did not have a license and from time to time, people would get hired and fired or brought in temporarily, but overall, the team started to rally around me. Being in that leadership role, I learned what it takes to have the pressure fall on you, to listen to the team's issues, and help the unit work through them. I learned that you build a culture before you build a business.

A few months later, they hired yet another person to take over but a month later, he was gone.

"You still good to take it on again?" I was asked.

"Sure thing," I said again.

I was back in the role. It was wild, and the whole time I was juggling college online to get my degree so that one day I could be the *official* Executive Director of the company.

Here I was, in school learning how to be a leader on paper when I was learning how to be a leader in person. I was hosting morning standup meetings; I was scheduling employees; I was learning cooking, nursing, and maintenance procedures to support the team as well as answering questions for the state survey. I was building marketing plans, and advertisements—then went from trying to close leads in sales to doing in-person medical assessments at the hospital to approve move-ins.

It is only new the first time you do something. When an opportunity is presented, even if it's something you've never done before, take a risk and give it your best effort. For me, it meant studying after work and in the early mornings. But what I learned with hands-on experience was unmatched—and it probably will be for you too. When we dive in, we more often than not make it work.

It was my job to move people into the building, but it became my responsibility to ensure the building was well run. I was rebuilding their reputation and couldn't let that slip.

But I was burning out.

After another few months and after passing a state survey without an official Executive Director in the building, another Executive Director was hired. Let's call her Karen.

Karen was awful. She started changing things up all over the place; no one could do right in her eyes. Any process that wasn't hers would be changed. Morning meetings would shift to afternoons, just to be different. Tour routes were "wrong" because she felt they should go differently; and how we accepted residents to our building required her approval only, because she wasn't about to take on anything that would cause her "problems."

Plus, she was sleeping around with the staff. One day, when I was giving a site tour to prospective clients, I literally "walked in" on her in one of our rooms (still managed to close that lead).

She made everyone feel like they weren't doing right; a real challenging boss. She was the type of person that would see the floors being mopped and would stop and say, "You missed this spot" even though the person wasn't done yet. I was done with the whole thing. Burned out.

Every other day I felt like I was going to lose my job.

It was bad.

In response, I told Jill I was going to quit, and she supported me.

So, the next day I went in to hand in my resignation, and this new Executive Director had a strict "no cell phone" policy.

She wouldn't so much as let you glance at your phone if you were in her presence, let alone ever text or talk on one.

I walked in and held up my letter of resignation. She was on *her* phone, so she gave me the one-finger raised high signal to "just wait"; her typical "power move" to show you she was in control and done so in a condescending manner.

So, there I was, standing there holding up my letter of resignation to someone who wouldn't give me the time of day when *my* phone rang. I knew her cell phone rules, all her rules, it was her way or the *wrong* way, and I said screw it.

I reached into my pocket and looked at the number. I didn't recognize it. I answered.

"Hello?"

The voice on the other end asked if I was "available."

In response, I told him the exact situation of my life at that present moment.

"Well, that's fantastic," he exclaimed, "because I'm looking to hire you." Elation welled up in me, a sign that I was doing the right thing.

I gave a nod to the universe and dropped my letter of resignation on the table before walking out the door to continue talking on my phone.

The guy on the other end was from a company we'll call Escapade Senior Living. They were in the same field of "retirement living" I had been in, and they were opening up in Reno.

They kept hearing about me somehow and had been making a point to reach out. We ended the call and I drove straight over, straight over to interview for a new job after tendering my resignation from another.

Sometimes things happen right on time—and in business, like in life, we can't ever forget that. Nature favors the bold. It is when we "go and do" that things seem to appear.

Once again, I was faced with the challenge to stay in a position to gain "success" or stepping away into the unknown, with no job, and no clue what was next to find MY SUCCESS.

I took the leap of faith, and before I could even realize what I was doing, I was again stepping out into another unknown.

30 IN 30

In 2009, Escapade Senior Living was a brand new, state-of-the-art thing. Apartment complexes for seniors where you can also gain access to high-end nursing services on the assisted living side, or memory care within a dedicated, secured area. Restaurants onsite, housekeeping included. Sometimes even a movie theatre or an arcade.

These were top of the line buildings, and I get hired with no experience.

I had to "sell the beds," which meant I was selling nothing less than apartments. A year's rent was forty to eighty thousand dollars. It was a little different than selling a pair of Jordans to a dude who liked hoops and hip hop.

But it also wasn't *that* different. Just like how that kid could've bought other, less expensive shoes, so could my new clients with how they chose to live out their last years.

But Jordans are on point, and Escapade apartments were too. While there was a cost, I knew there was *value*—I had to help some folks see that.

I was hired and I went straight to work. We were opening a new location, but time was tight. Usually, a new building was allowed seven to nine months to prep and plan and populate. They only gave us about ninety days. The team they had in place before this all walked out.

This meant I had almost no leads and zero time to hit my marks.

I developed a networking strategy and processes that had been ripped off and reused within the industry. Rebuilding my marketing plan, I set the foundation for MY SUCCESS. I identified the target market and the value prop of the brand and product. I designed campaigns to initial invites and tours, and I then used metrics to target the right people at the right time.

I got to work. With a budget of next to nothing, I knew that I was only going to accomplish this by "spending my time," and boy did I ever. Every waking moment was either used studying or applying what I was learning. I was out building relationships and connecting with people. The process I used to build my network was:

1. Develop community awareness through in-person meetings. Connect with every B2B professional that matches our primary referral type. Set one-on-one meetings to connect. Build the relationship. Start discovering how we can partner.

2. Connect to the community through both off and on-site events. Off-site, I was volunteering my time to support every event possible, then in return asking those people to join and support my events. On-site meant holding everything from hard-hat tours to lunches. I created a consistent approach toward getting everyone into our buildings to talk about us in the community. If someone would listen, I was pitching my product to them.

3. Use the relationships I've built to expand our events. Our community events would be explosive, having fifty to a hundred attendees versus the industry average of between five and twenty.

When building a new product, everyone has value. Build the largest database of people that you can, continue to grow and expand and ensure everyone knows who you are and what you offer. It's extremely time-consuming but gives each person the proper time to build a relationship. The return on this investment will carry over for years. Networking properly leads to the lifelong relationships that outlast short sales pitches.

I was a 24-year-old kid working with lifers, people two to four decades older than me who had done nothing else but this one single career track. They had all the experience in the world. I had none, but I knew I could connect with people. So that's where I started.

When we opened new buildings, they hosted a grand opening event. The goal was to bring the best salespeople to those galas to get the most move-ins, right then, on day one. As salespeople, we got a two and a half thousand dollar commission per move-in. That was on top of my pay and would really help pay off some debt.

Connect to people, I kept telling myself, *and get a lot of move-ins.*

My boss called me in shortly before a big grand opening and informed me about some conference call we had to make. He asked me if I had my numbers for the month ready.

"I do," I told him. We jumped on the call and after introductions and some shop-talking, my Regional Director asked me how many move-ins I am going to achieve.

"I'm going to do 28 move-ins," I said.

Everyone on the call started laughing. I didn't get what was so funny. Then, the COO spoke up. "28, huh? Why not make it 30? 30 in 30 days."

"Alright, I'll commit to thirty," I replied, confidently.

The laughter came again.

What I didn't know is that the best buildings, those that were "crushing it," get about eight move-ins in a month. I just said that I could do 30.

The call ended and it swiftly became an ongoing joke. I was now the "30 move-ins guy."

The sister property in another state had a grand opening before mine, and it was expected for all salesmen to participate, so I was invited to the event. It was frustrating, though, because I wouldn't receive commissions at the event. After all, it wasn't my property. But for me, I knew it was a valuable *experience* I could use to make my own event even better.

I flew out to Idaho where we had another meeting right before the event. They asked me, "So Billy, how many people are you going to get to give you fifty thousand dollars today?"

I knew the top guy got three once. "I'll do eight," I said. "Eight in one day."

I gave myself a challenge and be damned what others think. Let's go! I showed up at the site at 4:30 in the morning and started planning out my tour, getting to know the building inside and out since I'd never been to this one before.

The day started and I went hard: hustling, thinking, connecting. I gave site tours from eight a.m. to ten at night. I was having success, going nonstop with no breaks, and I continued to build relationships versus attempting to sell. Only after the relationship was built and the time was right did I ask for the sale.

I didn't care that I wouldn't make any commission—the sun was long down, I was on my last tour of the day, and I was tired, but screw it. I created the energy within, and I exuded it.

We connected and I closed. She gave me a deposit on the spot.

It was awesome. I walked down into the dining room and one of my Regional Directors saw that I just closed.

"Don't feel too bad, at least you got one, Billy," she said as the room of salespeople started laughing.

I had let them keep their little mid-game scoreboard thing going all day while I kept all my deposits in my binder.

"Actually, that's my eighth," I said, and I dropped down all the checks on the table so they could see for themselves.

As silence fell upon the room and jaws were dropping, I just left. Exhausted but satiated, I walked back to my hotel room. I wasn't there for the praise. I wasn't there for *their* version of success. I was there to learn what I needed to learn so I could change my life.

Right before I was set to fly home, the COO called me in and said that we need to talk about my commission structure. Most of their employees were lucky to get four commissions a month. I'd just brokered eight deals in one day, all without making a penny; they started to take me seriously. It seemed like they thought I could actually do thirty deals in one month, but the trouble was that they'd set the structure so high because they thought it would never be met.

What they really said is that if I sold 30 beds in 30 days, they didn't want to pay me the seventy-five thousand dollars they'd owe me.

To help their cause, they told me that I'd not only have to close the deals - get the money for them - but that everyone I brokered would also have to be physically moved in by the end of the month, or they wouldn't pay me.

I knew it was shenanigans, but I accepted it anyway. I knew they'd just set me up to fail, but I was going to prove them wrong and just do it. That's what I told myself. I would just keep showing these haters how narrow their vision was, that impossible was a frame of mind.

With a moving van or two coming and going every single day, I got 36 clients sold and moved in 30 days.

I broke a record, and it felt great, shattering their original record of 12 in a month. They'd have to pay me now.

I got the check.

The check was for seven grand.

The check was essentially missing an extra zero (they talked about the fine print and red tape and in the end, their way was the way it went. I never learned how they managed that one). They'd lied to me and told me to challenge them in court if I didn't like it. No way I could have done that, not with our debt.

They lied to me about money. That hurt. I was crushed.

I showed up for work at that job for a couple of weeks more, but there was nothing left in the tank. I'd worked myself to utter exhaustion for this company, and they weren't keeping their end of the bargain. The sad part was that I was setting up for another month of at least twenty more move-ins, but I didn't have it in me anymore. I was burned out, again.

The sea of bad was closing in on the island of good.

I left Escapade but ended up in the same industry. The executive director got poached by another senior living company that we'll call Interlude Retirement.

He took my playbook and regurgitated it all over the company.

The Playbook was a highly detailed and easy-to-follow marketing/ sales strategy guide I created to break records. I would customize a Playbook for each situation and tailor it to fit the marketing strategy. It was a document that was batched for strategy alignment and accountability for all those involved. It ensured that an entire location could do what I did and find success.

Here is one of my Playbooks—a 16-week program developed around direct mail advertising that's made organizations millions just by following these processes.

The Playbook

A Sales Playbook is a documented guide containing information and experiences on the most successful ways to sell your product. The Sales Playbook is not simply about your sales process but is the accumulated wisdom of reps, managers, marketing staff, and others who have had experience selling to your customers.

It is an ever-growing repository of experiences, successes, tactics, and strategies. With a Sales Playbook, new reps can focus on each new lead that is generated while following and understanding each week's next marketing plan for a complete 16-week ramp-up.

- In this playbook, you will see the direct mailing marketing plan for the next 16 weeks. Each event is outlined in the summary to begin preparations. The playbook uses a strategic blend of Incentives Pushes, Audience Targets, Referral Generation, and Open Houses to support you in the lead generation.

- Each week is outlined for Postcard Focus /Call Focus, the delivery date of all postcards, and specific event weekends to begin planning for. Each week's focus points will support you for each mailing to work towards the full effect of the strategic plan. Use these helpful tools to help generate each new lead for your community.

- *In your lead generation, Always* **LISTEN, FOCUS,** *and above all,* **DISCOVER** *every lead.*

LISTEN – Learn all you can about the lead. (How did you hear about us? What made you start thinking about purchasing the product? Tell me more about yourself.) Ask questions that will start a conversation that focuses on the lead and allows them to talk.

FOCUS – As you *listen* and learn about the lead, simplify the conversation to contour the conversation to the products and advantages. Pay attention to their wants, needs, and barriers.

DISCOVER – Through *listening and focusing* on the lead's wants, needs, and preferences you will learn **WHO** the lead is, **WHAT** they are looking for in retirement living, and **WHERE** they see themselves living, (such as size, location, expectations, etc.) **WHY** they are interested in the product and finally, **HOW** to close the lead. As you *DISCOVER* the lead, they will always tell you their wants, needs, and barriers that need to be overcome to close the deal.

Accompanying this, would be a calendar of events and the correlation of the direct mail drops.

PLAYBOOK CALENDAR OF EVENTS

16 Week Direct Mail / Event Program

	SUN	MON	TUES	WED	THURS	FRI	SAT
Week 1		New Mailing Lists	Direct Mail Drop Date	Estimated Delivery Dates **"Intro to Product"**			
Week 2							
Week 3			Direct Mail Drop Date	Estimated Delivery Dates **"Incentive Coupon"**			
Week 4							
Week 5			Direct Mail Drop Date	Estimated Delivery Dates **"Lead Targeted Marketing"**			
Week 6		New Mailing Lists		Estimated Delivery Dates **"Professional Referral Mailing"**			*Lead Targeting Event #1*
Week 7	*Lead Targeting Event #1*		Direct Mail Drop Date	Estimated Delivery Dates **"Open House Mailing"**			Profes-sionals Open House
Week 8						*Event 1 Lead Open House*	*Event 1 Lead Open House*
Week 9	*Event 1 Lead Open House*	New Mailing Lists	Direct Mail Drop Date	Estimated Delivery Dates **"Product Demo Event"**			
Week 10							
Week 11	*Product Demo Event*		Direct Mail Drop Date	Estimated Delivery Dates **"Lead Targeted Marketing #2"**			
Week 12							*Lead Targeting Event #2*

Week 13	*Lead Targeting Event #2*		Direct Mail Drop Date	Estimated Delivery Dates **"Competitor Mailing"**			
Week 14							
Week 15			Direct Mail Drop Date	Estimated Delivery Dates **"Incentive Mailing #2"**			
Week 16						*Event 2 Weekend*	*Event 2 Weekend*
Week 17	*Event 2 Weekend*						

OVERVIEW:

Marketing Summary

Week 1 – Intro to Product

Week 3 – Inventive Coupon Mailing

Week 5 – Lead Targeted Mailing

Week 6 – Professional Mailing

Week 7 – Open House

Week 9 – Product Demo Mailing

Week 10 – Internal Referral Push (No Mailing)

Week 11 – Lead Targeted Mailing

Week 13 – Competition Targeting

Week 15 – Incentive Mailing #2

Event Summary

Week 6 – Lead Targeting Event 1

Week 7 – Professionals Open House

Week 8 – Lead Open House

Week 12 – Lead Targeting Event 2

Week 17 – Lead Targeting Event 3

This program was a way to track, to hold those involved accountable, and it gave a continual approach to marketing that was non-stop for the entire 16 weeks. I also built strategies around supporting veterans, discovering that there were programs designed to give senior veterans the support to live in senior living. We made amazing changes to support our vets - many of whom were homeless or otherwise struggling - and changed how many of them were able to take part in high-level senior living.

After hearing that I was the creator of the Playbook, Interlude quickly recruited me. It was like I was traded to another team, or better, "picked up off the waiver wire."

It was another chance at sales. Another chance to play some ball and take care of my family, so I took it—of course I did. I was just trying to hold on. I had no idea about self-care, didn't know the term existed, and wouldn't have known what to do with it if I did. I was all-go all the time. I felt like I had to work to live but, as I look back now, all that work was leading me toward an early grave. I was a slave to those above me.

I was in the rat race so deep I couldn't see anything over the walls that life built up for me.

Now, at the age of 25, I was responsible for a one hundred million dollar portfolio.

Part Six

"To succeed in baseball, as in life, you must make adjustments."

- Ken Griffey Jr.

'THE KID'

So, back to the through-line: Interlude Retirement heard about me somehow and signed me on. At the time, they were trying to grow into this monster, so they were grabbing every person in the industry, paying them well, and growing. Once again, I found myself as easily the youngest person in the room. Pretty early on, I started to get a nickname: The Kid.

I liked it. My favorite baseball player growing up was Ken Griffey Jr. His nickname was "The Kid" too. Griffey was drafted right out of high school and made the jump to the majors when he was still a teenager.

I always thought it was cool, being the youngest. Like it made me different, like I saw things a little differently than those around me, and like I had the energy to follow through on what I saw.

When Interlude hired me, they sent me straight off to the home office in Pacific Northwest for training. They'd been going through a transition; they'd finally seen some things and were bringing on people from all walks of life and ages to grow the industry. So, the majority of people coming in were from outside the industry—a lot of them didn't know senior living from sustainable living.

At this point, I'd already run skilled nursing and opened my own building to high success. I knew my stuff.

I flew up to the meeting. It was supposed to be a two-week training session for every new Regional Director that comes into the business. I arrived there and as per usual everyone was ten to fifteen years older than me.

I walked into the first sales and marketing meeting and sat down. They started asking me questions, and I started answering. The questions were like child's play. I knew all the answers. Most of the folks in the room had never sold senior living, I felt pretty far ahead of the game. They started asking how I tour a potential lead. As I began to explain my process, these "trainers" started taking notes.

Then, the lead trainer looked up at me and stammered out, "you know more than I do about this..."

I kind of half apologized.

They called up my boss: "Hey, your guy knows everything. Why is he here?"

Long story short, they decided they were going to move me away from marketing and sales and into operations training so I can start to learn how to be a Regional Director of Operations.

They put me in executive operations, and I was with Regional Operational Directors. Now, the age difference was super drastic. Everyone here was even older. I walked into the room and stood out like a sore thumb. These are the powerhouse players.

The CEO, Keith, came in, gave his speech, and then walked over and noticed me (because who wouldn't notice a kindergartener in a high school class). He came up to me and is like, "Who are you?"

"I'm Billy Thompson, the new Regional Director of Marketing and Sales for California," I said, as though I'd been practicing in front of a mirror, really excited to meet this guy, the first real executive I'd ever really met and introduced myself to.

His look lingered on me. "What are you doing in this meeting?"

I looked up at him, blank-faced.

"You are in sales and marketing," he told me. "You're not *capable* of being in this meeting."

The energy that Keith, this high-powered executive, was wielding over me was overwhelming. He just stared at me, almost daring me to say something. It was like I was in the principal's office. I began shaking, like *what?*

Finally, I told him the story of how I ended up being sent to this room. "I don't know what I've done to offend you," I stammered, "but I am sorry."

Didn't work. Keith was basically like, get your stuff and get out of this room.

Okay. I gave him a"Yes, sir" and grab my stuff. I walked out of the room like I am told, but Keith walked out with me, escorting me back to where he thought I belonged, so I wouldn't skip class.

"I don't know what game you're trying to play," he said, "but at Interlude, we have a process."

He took me back to the training room specifically for marketing and signaled me to sit while he walked up to the trainer and whispered something into her ear. Everyone in class was looking at me like, "who is this Billy guy?"

It's fine, I told myself. *I can jump back from this. I can.*

Other than the thoughts in my head, I was trying to stay quiet. I didn't want to be noticed, didn't want to speak up in class. So, I didn't. But the trainer called on me anyway, maybe wanting to show me how I really didn't know as much as I thought. "Billy," she says, "why don't you come on up and explain how a tour works." *Tours.* Yeah, in the room I had just been put back into, they were teaching the basics of how to give a site tour. I had just sold 36 beds in a month!

I got up out of my chair and walked up to the front of the class as the instructor had asked me to. I thought I was about to redeem myself, about to show this whole operation what a rock star I was. I walked up to the front and started to teach, started telling them how I gave site tours, and some of the tools of the trade that helped me achieve the sales records that I had.

Shortly into me beginning my speech, the trainer left the room. I didn't really know why she did that, but I guessed that it was a vote of confidence that I could run the class for a couple of minutes while she went to the bathroom or something.

Not so much.

About a minute later, she walked back in. With Keith. Both were fuming. Keith pointed at me, and then he pointed out the door.

"I'm so done," I told myself, and I walked back out of the room.

I got out into the hallway, and again Keith was asking me who I thought I was?!

He proceeded to tell me that the instructor had just come out and informed him that I had "taken over the class." Keith already thought that I was a troublemaker; I felt cornered and started to sweat, my heart beat faster. I was not exactly sure how the rest of the conversation went but it ended with him telling me to sit in the back of the room and keep my mouth shut or I would lose my job.

Then he stormed off.

My mind was a complex mix of fog and fire as I returned to the classroom and took my seat in the far back. A couple of questions were posed by the trainer that I knew the answers to, but I kept my mouth shut.

I never raised my hand or spoke up. Not once.

But she still called on me. "Billy?"

"Oh, sorry, don't know that one." But I *did* know. And it felt like a box. I felt constrained but I needed the job. I needed it for my family. I couldn't mess it up, so I kept my mouth shut.

For about four days.

On day five, they took our class out to a physical location to do some test site tours. We did some roleplay, where the trainer acted as the "seller" and one of the trainees was the "client."

After several people had a crack at it, the trainer called my name to come up and do the routine with her.

I object, but she said that I had to come up and help. Tentatively, I walked up to the front of the class and did what the trainer asked. I went along with her fake sales pitch as her fake client, trying to make her look good in front of the class.

At the end of her textbook spiel, she turned to the class.

"You see guys, that's how you handle a sale."

Thing was, her pitch was awful, and I just wanted to get out of the situation and back to the back of the class where I could be quiet and not get fired. But before I could, one of the students raised their hand.

"I don't mean to offend you—but why didn't you just ask for the sale?"

The class erupted in laughter, his question obviously spoke for more of the students than just himself.

The trainer started bawling her eyes out. No joke, she started crying and ran out of the room.

"I'm screwed," I said.

And, yep, a couple of minutes later the door ripped open and slamed hard against the wall. It was Keith again. He pointed at me, again. Then he pointed out the door, again.

He walked me down to his office and sat me down in this massive chair in his enormous executive office. I felt like a toddler in that chair—like somehow my feet couldn't reach the ground.

"You're disrupting my training," Keith fumed.

"She asked me to come up and demonstrate!" I said, protesting my innocence.

"You think you know so much about this industry, huh? You're just a kid. You don't know anything and you think you could teach this class?" He asked in an accusatory manner. Everything about his body language was confrontational. But I stood by my guns.

"Yes sir, I do."

Now Keith was really fuming. He was like, "If I hear you open your mouth just one more time…!"

I was both intimidated by this guy and I did not like this guy. He finally excused me, and I walked out. I grabbed my phone and called my new boss, Matt.

Matt answered and I told him I had to quit.

"What do you mean?" he said, confused.

I explained the situation. "If I'm in this room for one more minute I'm going to get fired anyway."

Matt tried to placate me by telling me how pointless the training was anyway.

"Just go to your hotel and pack your stuff up and jump on a flight back out to California. I'll call them and make up some excuse. Forget the training. Let's get to work."

That's Matt for you—always willing to cut through the nonsense and get straight to business. Matt was leaps and bounds above everyone in this company. His concepts for running a minimum loss region were saving the company millions while everyone else spent money and lost clients like they grew on trees.

Matt is good people, he's also part of my crew, my mentor. Instantly I knew this man was a leader, someone I respected, looked up to, and still do.

I hung up the phone and ditched the rest of the training. I walked out of the home office, went to the hotel, packed my gear, and flew down to California to meet up with Matt.

And I wore my ballcap backward, just like Ken Griffey Jr.—if I was going to be treated like a kid, then you can be damn sure I was going to embrace it.

I got down to Cali and it fast became a whirlwind. From day one, I was sitting in on big meetings. Right before a giant one, Matt said, "Billy, I need you to run this meeting. You can handle it." He told me to introduce myself and meet the crew—and then to pitch my marketing strategy for the year.

It was my first meeting, and he wanted me to get up in front of everyone and go for it like that? "Sure thing."

We drove out to Napa—yes, *that* Napa. Wine country. Vineyards as far as the eye could see. We drove out to one of our sites and all the managers and staff were there; fifty to a hundred people in this tiny room. Everyone else in the room was in their forties or fifties and I'm Ken Griffey Jr. just trying to make a play out in the center.

I got up and started the meeting, and I was right in the middle of it when one of the managers stood up out of his chair and said: "Yeah—why do I have to listen to you?"

I didn't really know how to answer the question, so I looked over to Matt, but he was just leaning back in his chair, all nonchalant, looking at me. I read his eyes, read his micro-expressions, and he was saying, "Well, kid, let's see what you can do."

It was a look you only see a few times in your life, a look of ascension, and I'm glad I recognized it. I'd been getting the crap kicked out of me lately, and I wasn't about to get the crap kicked out of me again.

I looked at the guy and took a step forward and answered his question.

"Because I'm the person who decides if you have a job at the end of the day, that's why."

His jaw dropped a little and he kind of just looked at me, shocked, and he finally sat down and let me continue.

Even as "The Kid" - perhaps *because* I was "The Kid" - I felt like I had to go in and assert some dominance. If you are just starting in your career and working hard and competing against others, sometimes you just gotta be able to say "this is how this is."

At least every once in a while.

For my young readers: age doesn't matter, work ethic and dedication do. There is a reason they batch entire articles around thirty under thirty each year:

1. It is possible to do what someone older cannot.
2. Few walk this path.

For those young entrepreneurs wanting to change the world, do not allow the world to tell you that you're too young. If you can achieve success, your age will disappear. I say embrace the critics and prove them wrong with actions, not words. Put in the effort, stay positive, remain motivated, and embrace being the "kid" in the room with a big smile.

I went through a couple of days and I was reaching the end of my first work week. And, of all the times on the planet, I woke up on Thursday and I was sick as a dog. Like, sicker than I'd ever been in my life. We were out on the road and I was down with a bad flu. I told myself I had to work. Couldn't call in sick, not that day, not ever.

I was up all night, throwing up, fevered, chilled, and sick as hell. I got up and splashed some water on my face and got to work.

Matt could tell how sick I was. I was miserable and just fighting through the day. We had been driving site-to-site and I wasn't improving in the slightest. After one site and before another we rolled up to a gas station.

"Need anything, Matt?" I said.

"What we need is for you to get some medicine."

I told him I couldn't afford any.

He was dumbfounded.

He had been making over a hundred thousand dollars per year for years. But we shared another look that I'll always remember, a look of empathy.

"Don't worry about." he said, "I got you, I'm paying for it."

I walked into the store and grabbed some NyQuil and such to help me get through that week. I think I earned a lot of respect for how hard I worked, and for how far I pushed my body and mind. I didn't know how unhealthy it was, but somehow, I made it through.

I know it's not healthy to work through being sick—but, to go beyond ("Plus Ultra" for the anime fans out there), I felt like I had no choice but to go at this pace.

THE GRIND

Our Managing Director at Interlude expected hundred hour-plus weeks: grueling. As a result, I was out on the road in different cities all the time.

I routinely woke up at 5am, probably having gone to bed around two that morning. I would get ready in my hotel room, shower quickly, ensure my dress shirt was pressed and wrinkle-free, and be down in the lobby to meet Matt for breakfast (breakfast was important because I knew I might not have another meal until seven or eight that evening, at the earliest). Then we'd drive straight out to the community and work all day. No breaks, no food, non-stop all day, doing interviews, meeting with residents and staff, training, tours, helping salespeople close deals, and so on.

We'd grab some sort of dinner on the way back to the hotel, typically sushi or some random steak house-type place. We wouldn't linger long because we both knew our workday wasn't done yet. It was back to the lobby to build marketing and sales strategies and figure out what our region was going to do for the month. We usually went well past midnight, then I'd grab what sleep I could and wake up at five to do it all again.

We'd repeat this again and again. Six days a week, out on the road, and away from my family, all at the mercy of my employer, my job literally working me into the ground.

I'd get home Saturday afternoon and see Ren and Jill, and then pass out and stay asleep most of Sunday. If I had it in me, we'd have good family time on Sunday evenings, but even that was rare. We tried our best, but I was just so tired. I'd only truly get to see them for a few hours before that alarm rang on Monday morning and I'd start up the insane cycle again.

The pace was unbelievable. The pace was unrealistic. But I had monumental debt. And I'd made a promise that I was going to pay it off. MY SUCCESS was making enough money to pay it off, and the only way to do that, I felt, was to keep on grinding as hard as I could. I was on commission and so I needed to sell. I was going to grow my region to reach these heights.

That was my goal, and Matt supported me fully in this.

"What do you need?" he would ask, and then he would provide me with it. We worked our tails off every month to hit our goals, but it just didn't matter how well we performed; we always felt like we were about to lose our jobs. It was not a healthy workplace. We would be number one in sales one month, then the following month be told that if we didn't "get our numbers up," we were both fired. We would save six clients from leaving the product, and we'd get asked why we "couldn't get seven?"

Nothing was ever good enough. The emotional abuse the company put on us was unfathomable. I mean, it was insane.

The only good thing was becoming so close with Matt. He was the first person I saw when I woke up in the morning, and the last person I saw before I went to bed at night. If he was on the phone when the server came to our table at the restaurant, I'd just order for him based on his attitude that day—and he always said I got it right. We definitely formed a bond, probably because it felt like we were partners in a survival situation.

It was crazy, the environment we were in, how we were being treated, the sheer number of hours and human life we were giving to "the job." Mental health wasn't really talked about back then, but I'll tell you that we all had mental health issues. Big ones, all of us. But no attention was paid to it—not by us and definitely not by higher ups. The whole thing was just chaos. From the top down, it was chaos.

When you're up twenty-plus hours a day working six days straight, everything kind of starts to blur together, but the blur does not go by quickly. The year I spent working for Interlude was the longest year of my life. During this time, I had to go to the hospital for work exhaustion—not once, not twice, but *three* times.

The amount of my life that my work was requiring was not worth it, but I saw no other way to make money and pay off that debt. I wasn't working smart, just hard. Just sweat and toil. It was all I knew back then.

I was trying to sprint a marathon, which isn't possible. If you remember your Greek history, the task flat-out killed the first guy who ever tried it. After the Greeks had prevailed in the Battle of Marathon, the guy ran the 26.2 miles back home as fast as he could to tell the others. After he delivered his message, he keeled over.

But I was still trying to sprint a marathon in my own way, always. I had yet to learn how to work smarter toward MY SUCCESS. All I knew was how to work harder, toward *their* success. Although hard work is required in pursuing our goals, killing ourselves to reach them is not. I was trapped in the lie, trapped in a rigged game that I was bound to lose. The world is going to tell you that in order to get promoted or whatever, you must work as many hours as you possibly can.

Wrong.

I am telling you that this game is rigged. I am telling you to make new rules for a new game.

Define what will make *you* happy. Define what will bring *you* peace. Define YOUR SUCCESS.

And then chart your course and set sail.

Burnout is reaching a point of consistent stress that ultimately leads to feeling disconnected from life, exhaustion, and feeling useless or ineffective. It can show up in other ways too such as with insomnia, anxiety, fatigue, forgetfulness, lack of concentration, depression, and self-isolation. Having these hit you should be the alert to STOP and reflect on what you're doing in life personally and professionally.

We can all burn out from either side, and each side can be a contributing factor. SUCCESS comes from finding self-balance. You need to continually find a balance in your life. As you add more stress, you need to balance this by adding more personal care to your life.

CLOSING LEADS

When I started at Interlude, they had me take a personality test. There was some mix-up with it, and so they had me take another one.

I took the first test in the comfort of my own home. I was pretty relaxed and after I answered the questions, it told me that my natural personality was an introvert and a follower. That's how I was built and if I have a choice, I prefer to stay quiet. To those who analyzed the test, my results told them that I was a terrible leader and that I would rather follow because I didn't have much of an authoritative stance.

The second test, however, I took when I was out at the company office getting the crap kicked out of me. During the bombardment, my personality had flipped, that survival switch in my brain being flipped on, and it changed my mentality to an extrovert who wants to take charge. If I'm being challenged, if someone says, "you can't do this," I bare down and go seek out ways to prove them wrong. It's a reflex. So, the test results from this one showed that by their markers, I excelled in all levels of leadership, especially in challenging situations.

The results of the two tests were polar opposites. When the head of HR saw this, they started to accuse me of cheating on the test because no one by their lens could display such diverse flips. I also found out that this guy was also responsible for creating the test, which may have played into his reaction.

And that's where I dove even deeper into psychology, learning how to apply it to my own brain. I started to understand the hows and whys behind the way I was acting in certain situations. When I started to understand myself better, I started to be able to control my flips and alter my leadership behavior according to the different roles I was being asked to play.

When my extrovert/leader characteristics were triggered, my whole demeanor and body language changed too. When I was relaxed and at ease, my tone, inflection, and mannerisms were much different. It kind of reminded me of octopi; how they can change colors and textures depending on if they are hunting or being hunted.

But I still didn't know how to apply all of what I was learning. So, after the head of HR looked at my two different tests, they began trying to decide if I should be demoted from regional to just a single site because I wasn't "mentally capable" of running this region. They derived this from those tests—not from my performance or real life, but from those answers to questions on a piece of paper.

They called me up and told me as much and it ticked me off. I took it as a challenge, and I decided to throw down. But positively. I went and spoke with Matt "What's the record number of move-ins for one weekend in this company?" I asked him.

"Six."

"I can do ten," I said.

I was amped. I wanted to show what I could do. My extrovert/ leader had been triggered.

I brought out my sales staff and put together a strategy—we were going to spend some money and put on the best weekend event of all time. Matt even took me down to Office Depot and bought Adobe Illustrator. I taught myself how to use it. I came back the next week as our designer (to avoid having to wait for our home office, which could take months), and I designed the event—all the flyers, direct mail, door hangers, banners, and advertisements. I even placed all the ads and sent them out.

We created a ton of buzz for the event, and I was excited. Saturday morning came around and it was huge. There was a veritable sea of people: the event was kicking off before we were even supposed to be open. *Perfect,* I thought, *volume in the pipeline.*

But no one was closing deals.

It was the first day of our two-day event, and everyone was having a great time, the building looked great, but no one was closing. We'd spent a ton of money on this shindig, and we needed to start getting some dang deposits.

As the day started drawing to a close, I took another look around, a hint of panic setting in, and thought that maybe we'd done too much, put on too much of a show and that it looked staged or something… too formal maybe.

I got an idea and look at Matt.

"Don't come into work tomorrow," I told him.

He didn't understand. I asserted to him that I didn't want him to walk into this building until three o'clock.

"Why?"

"Because I'm going to close some leads," I said, "my way."

I knew what I needed to do, this was my responsibility now.

That, and I also knew that Matt's daughter had a basketball game. Matt deserved to be there for her. He needed to be at her game, and I needed to handle this event.

I came in the next day and was not wearing the suit and tie I was on Saturday. Although required by the company, that was too formal. That was not me. I walked in wearing a simple T-shirt and jeans. I was here to *connect* with people, so I showed up how I would if I was going to go hang out with my friends. I felt good, my mind was sharp, and I was confident: *me* with no pretenses, just Billy Thompson.

I met with my staff. I would teach them "my way".

"Every person that you tour but don't close, drop them back off with me at this doorstep so I can tour them again. We'll work leads together to increase the close ratios." I explained. This wasn't a typical approach, it could be too pushy and cost you the lead for a later date. I needed to take things into my hands, my way, the way I knew would work.

The day began. People were psyched. A couple of deposits were finally taken, but a lot of tours still went off without a close, and every one of those prospective clients was dropped back off with me at the doorstep—and I re-toured every single person one more time.

I did this in my simple T-shirt and jeans, making authentic connections, and when Matt showed up that afternoon at three, I had a line of twenty people waiting to sign contracts with him. The challenge brought out the best in me. It flipped my switch. Again. We closed twenty-eight people that weekend.

The president of the company called me up later that night at the hotel. He called me up to personally thank me for the amount of revenue I'd just generated. I'd spent ten thousand dollars on the weekend, and - based on the average length of stay for these residents - we brought in millions in revenue.

If things worked out like I thought they should, I knew my commission check would be a life-changer.

Throughout the next week, I checked my email early and often. Tons of emails, but not the one I was looking for. Then, later in the week, I pulled open my phone and logged into my email, and there it is in the inbox. I hesitated a moment, scared, thoughts of Escapade all over again.

I managed to click open the email and looked at the screen. I see numbers and a dollar sign. They'd treated me honestly. My commission for one month, for one weekend really, was what I almost used to make in an entire year. I walked into the bedroom and woke up Jill to show her the dollar amount. She broke down into tears.

Debt is over. And our life is about to take off.

It's easy to sit here and talk about my successes. But it wasn't all success. Creating my perfect sales event took time and planning. This short section doesn't cover the hours spent in development leading up to creating this event. As you learn your industry, start small. Take the time to test different sales techniques, advertising avenues, and closing processes.

Once you get a grasp on your target market, audience, and goals, you can begin to formulate a plan. Use the small tests to determine the highest success rates, then reapply to those areas only. As the formula proves true again, you're ready to begin expanding into larger events. If the event fails, this can be used for success as well. Learn from everything you applied and continue to move forward.

Part Seven

"Just because you put syrup on something don't make it pancakes."

- Shawn Spencer, Psych

MORE!

When you make a company millions of dollars in one weekend, they want you to replicate it.

They wanted me to run an event every weekend.

"You know how much work that is?!" I lamented to Jill out on our patio.

And, of course, the head of HR had his two cents. He was happy with the revenue, sure, but then was like, "I can't have you receiving recognition right now. Matt, you have to take credit for this event."

"I wasn't even there?" Matt said, "This was all Billy."

Our Managing Director in essence told Matt, sternly, that he was going to take the credit. Then he hung up and Matt and I just looked at each other. I could see the conflict in him.

"It's okay, I'm good with it." I assured him.

Honestly, it didn't bother me. Success before ego, right? Recognition was becoming less and less of value as I further defined MY SUCCESS. As long as they paid those commission checks, I was fine with it. I was building something much more valuable than awards and accolades. I needed to chart a course, one that wasn't on their map, but mine.

And how was I doing it? Well, it was a simple premise—stop pretending and just ask.

Most people in marketing like to hide what they are offering, almost making it a game or mystery to discover for the lead to figure out. Me, I like to tell my leads *exactly* what is going on. As I mentioned earlier, I do not force a sale and I do not sell to people that don't want or need my product. So, I just focused on highly targeted marketing. I built a mailing list based on that target.

I ran an analysis of the last six months of people that purchased my product. I interviewed them, learned their habits, and profiled them. After breaking down the data, I was able to see common trends: ages, areas they lived in prior to moving in, and preferences of how they liked being talked to. I knew we needed something dynamic, so in addition to the targeted direct mail, I took flyers to every business in town, pinned them throughout the city, then went door-to-door and placed door hangers on each-and-every door within a five-mile radius of the location—specifically hitting areas with a high concentration of seniors.

It all led to a real "Move-In Mania." The sheer amount of people at the event created a sense of urgency. We honestly couldn't guarantee to prospective clients that their perfect room would still be available by the end of the day. We sold a bunch of beds and made a lot of money.

But, still, I did not get the credit. Matt - not me - started flying out across the country to teach people my method.

And it was weird, not getting the credit I deserved for my ideas was a common trend in my life and was for a long time.

Even now, when I consult, I still often don't get named or anything for my ideas. But it truly no longer matters. I can say that I've moved that far along my path. All I care about now, in that vein, is seeing my ideas make people money.

Still, before setting out on my own, the higher-ups at these companies didn't like a lot of the things I did. They saw my hustle and my ideas as some sort of threat. A lot of them made it known that they did not like me because I was accomplishing things that people had not previously accomplished.

A couple of weeks after my multi-million-dollar weekend, I was in the back of this meeting with another executive of the company. This guy was another high-powered top dog in the industry.

He leaned over to me: "So, you're the hotshot kid, huh?" he said, and he started pushing my buttons, like, how good *are* you?

"I'm the best closer in this company," I told him in a brash, cocky 25-year-old tone as I could tell he was pushing me.

"No one can outsell me."

He mulled some ideas over in his head as the meeting continued, then followed up.

"If you're such a hotshot, then how about we see you go close a deal. Right now?" I knew he was challenging me.

He threw out the name of a location, one that was struggling heavily over the past few months. "How about you go there and close a deal before the end of the day?"

He knew what he was asking was near-impossible. The average lead to close time could take weeks, it was near-impossible to just walk into a building and close a deal. Especially this location.

But, I took it as another challenge, a way to push myself. *More experience and training.*

He put out an agreement that if I closed a deal before the end of the day, I gained his respect, and an extra day off work.

"Deal." I said with zero hesitation.

I got up and rushed out of the meeting, I got in a car and drove the two hours out to the site. I parked and walked inside the building and it was a complete circus. They had a blend of salespeople fighting over leads, no one was accurately tracking leads in our Customer Relationship Management system (CRM), half the management team was taking a "personal day," and to top it off, it's cold as heck, and about to rain—not great for incoming tours.

"What leads do you have?" I asked the community manager.

"None."

I've just been summoned out of the bullpen like Mariano Rivera. I need to save the game.

"We're getting on the phone," I said as I rallied the team, "This comes from the top— we need to close a deal today. I need your help everyone. We can do this." I explained the situation, the team was ready to support me.

Everyone got out their phones and started making calls. Bunches of them, but nothing was happening. We were reaching the end of the day, and I looked at the clock on the wall. *I've got to close this game out*, I thought to myself.

And then, I watched as this middle-aged lady walked in. I performed a quick body language and micro-expression study. I could tell that she was stressed.

"I'm taking this one," I said to the team. A random walk-in—my favorite.

I gave her the greatest tour of my career. We became fast friends. I got to know who she was, and asked her why she was stressed and what she needed.

I got straight to the point. I also gave her a nice, late lunch as she hadn't eaten all day. After I'd shown her everything and made a connection with her, we sat down and really bonded. Plus, she was loving what I had to say about this building and the potential life within it for her mother.

Her only objection was that it was a bit far away from her house to travel to see her mother.

"I just worry about the cost of all that gas to get Mom moved in here," she explained, looking like this little fact was going to rain out her dreams of her mom living here.

I looked at her and smiled. I knew I had just the thing. I reached into my wallet and gave her a couple gas cards. I'd often hang onto these for moments like this, a small expense on my end.

She smiled, took the gas card, and signed the deal.

I closed the deal as easy as fielding a three-hopper at shortstop.

And then I drove back over and told the executive all about it.

There is a continual contradiction inside of me, an internal struggle. I'm sure you've faced similar. Push harder than you can imagine… but know your limit. Give 110 percent of yourself… but don't give up YOU. *It's a balance, so how do you figure out when to push and when to back off?*

You have to evaluate constantly. At the end of each day or the end of each week, take an hour to evaluate your successes and failures of the week (personally and professionally), start making a checklist of these moments to compare and contrast, and figure out the cost and value (we'll get into this a bit later) of your efforts and reflect on what you need to focus on finding YOUR SUCCESS.

OFF COURSE

Even though I was excelling at work, doing some dynamic things, and bringing home larger and larger paychecks, I just was not in existence in my daughter's life.

I was always gone, always out on the road away from Ren—out on the job, working. That was my life. I wanted to be the best husband and father I could be, but I wasn't doing it. All I was doing was grinding.

One day, I came home a bit early. I was ready to spend time with my Jill and Ren. I came through the door, excited to see Ren, but startled, she backed away. I called for her, arms outstretched, big smile. But there was fear in her eyes. She was acting like she would around a stranger.

My heart broke into a million pieces. I realized that my two year old didn't know who her father was. It was bad.

As I mentioned, my life at this point wasn't filled with much time at home. When I got home, I'd try my best to spend time with Ren and Jill, but I also needed as much sleep as I could. So, I was going straight to bed. During the week, I was averaging about two and a half hours of sleep a night.

At home I could get six or more. I developed a way where I could push, push, push, catch a few hours of rest, then go some more. Sleep wasn't part of the routine because while I slept I couldn't learn, research, or make money.

I knew every other person functioned optimally with eight hours of sleep, but somehow, I could get by with a couple of hours. I think it was how alert I always had to be as a kid, all that keeping my head on a swivel. I trained my body to be able to go without sleep for longer and longer stretches at a time.

I got to where I could go forty-eight hours straight without sleep—or food. Adrenaline and a need for making more money kept me grinding.

It was killing me.

It was killing my body, and it killed my spirit when my own daughter didn't recognize me that day.

Still, I couldn't seem to get my schedule under control. Work was taking everything from me, including my relationship with my daughter. I pushed so hard that my brain literally shut off one day. It was crazy.

I woke up in the hotel to my alarm at 5:30, just like every other day. I had an hour to get ready and out the door. I forced myself out of bed, took a shower, and checked my phone again. 5:45. I got dressed, packed up, and headed downstairs. On the elevator, I checked my phone—5:55.

I walked by the front desk and said "have a great day" to the clerk. She gave me a strange look, but I thought nothing of it. I continued on, ready to start my day.

Then I stepped outside.

I looked around.

It was pitch black.

I looked down at my phone again. I saw the 5:58 on the screen. I was on the East Coast, I thought—the sun should haven been up by now?

But then, like I was in a dream or something, the numbers started to blur, started to change, reformed before my very eyes—and now the digits on the phone read 1:58.

It wasn't 5:58 a.m., but 1:58 a.m. I'd only been asleep less than an hour. My burnout had become so severe that my mind had literally shut off.

I later learned that this rare psychological response must have been set off by a random sound—my mind heard something that sounded like my alarm and just reacted to it.

I had no idea what was going on. But I knew I had to start taking better care of myself.

Be careful, be careful, be careful. Some of you out there can work beyond, to go PLUS ULTRA, this is a great gift if you can control it. However, we will all reach a point where we go too far. You must reflect on your efforts at the end of each week. It is vital to remember that if you push too far, you'll get set back even further. If you were training for a weightlifting competition, tore a muscle, and kept going, what is your likely future? A deeper tear and losing the ability to compete. Take the time to reflect on your life and ensure you are taking care of yourself, and your mind, and getting what you need to recover.

Remember the balance scale, as stress increases you should search for ways to relieve that stress by balancing in additional things that bring you happiness.

RECONNECTED

Jill's grandfather, Bill, was a brilliant man. Throughout her life, stemming from her childhood, they were very close, and I spent a lot of time proving to him that I was worthy of her.

He was a man I respected and loved immensely, and his passing was a devastating loss for us all. To help Jill cope, I stayed at home for a few weeks. During this time, I got to be Dad again, but I also got to be a husband to my grieving wife.

Being "human" again felt nice, even despite the circumstances in which I was given the opportunity, and it spurred me to reminisce about what had occurred so far in my life. I was overcome with nostalgia, driven by the pain my family was feeling.

In my reminiscing, I got back in touch with old friends and acquaintances, mainly checking in to see how things had changed and to attempt to fill some of the gaps that had grown in my life.

I also got back in touch with Connect. I was curious, I wanted to see how they were doing. When I made the call, I was asked for some business advice on a possible restructuring of Connect.

I agreed to take a look and started a full evaluation. I ran the numbers and discovered how their cell phone revenue was slowly fading; not good for a store that focuses on selling cell phones. Based on my predictive models and research, the trend was looking bleak.

I looked it over again, double-checked the numbers, and saw that this business could be in real trouble, and fast.

I explained this to the owner.

"What?" he said in surprise, "but we're profitable."

I showed him the market trends. He was still primarily selling cell phones as an independent contractor.

"In five years, your type of store will be non-existent. They'll all be exclusive Verizon stores, AT&T stores, and T-Mobile stores. Smartphones are going to get more expensive. You won't be able to compete. You won't have the infrastructure to hold an inventory of what will be required," I explained in detail, holding back nothing.

The owner was a very smart entrepreneur, and he could see the numbers clearly. He asked me what I recommend he do.

I put together a plan. At the time, they were 90 percent cellular and 10 percent printing—business cards and letterhead for local businesses and such.

"If it was me," I concluded, "I would flip your model and move more toward the printing while phasing out the cellular."

"I don't know if I can do that," the owner said, "nor do I have the time by myself."

I taught him what he needed to know, giving insights on how to make such a transition and where to begin. Thus, I started my consulting career.

Walking through the processes, I conducted a review of the store and the team. It needed a full reconstruction. The products of print needed to dominate the cellular. I reviewed strategies and marketing plans to refocus on printing. The problem was, however, that there wasn't anyone capable of generating enough sales for the flip. Here's where things get interesting: I simultaneously get offered a job to consult in the senior living industry down in Phoenix. It was a great job—six figures, purely consulting, traveling three days a week, commission, profit share, and benefits. But I was worried about being away from home again. My number one goal was to be the best father I could be. How could I be a great father if I'm not even around? The pain of Ren forgetting my face was still raw.

I took a deep breath.

I needed to be a dad. This, I knew. The debt was gone, and I knew we could survive on a reduced income. In fact, I knew, for my family, we would *thrive* on less income if it meant I would be at home more often.

In addition, Jill had also been advancing, developing financial techniques that stretched our money like Jesus stretched a fish (she should definitely write a book on it). With her abilities, we had paid off all our debts and I knew we could make anything work.

After discussing with my Jill, we agreed on our next course in life. I walked away from that six-figure offer and rejoined the Connect team. I took a job at Connect for thirty thousand dollars a year, all so I could be home.

It was a defining moment in my journey toward MY SUCCESS. What are some of yours?

We all have a different form of SUCCESS. What might seem crazy to one person may be the perfect answer to another. I left a hundred thousand dollars to get thirty thousand, or as the expression goes, I stepped over a dollar to pick up a penny.

Considering this portion only, it would seem crazy. But my cost versus value had other factors to consider: my time at home, my health, my family, and pursuing MY SUCCESS. You should always take the time to evaluate and ensure you are on the path toward YOUR SUCCESS and do not let anyone steer you in a different direction.

NO MORE MOWING LAWNS

Once again, I had no clue what I was doing in my career. Here I was, taking a major step backward, going from what was over a hundred and twenty-five thousand dollars a year with commission, down to a job working for thirty thousand dollars.

I started mowing lawns in the evenings just to pay the bills. Not ideal, but I'll do anything for my family.

Going from traveling to a new city every day and staying at 5-Star hotels with fine dining (when I actually ate) to being hemmed into a single location was quite the adjustment. It was a hard adjustment. Managing millions of dollars to working with an annual revenue stream of three hundred thousand dollars; from managing roughly one thousand employees across ten locations to working with a team of four. Life had changed.

But I was home with my daughter and my Jill, and that was enough. So, I welcomed the change and the new challenge.

Transitioning Connect toward printing meant I needed to rethink the whole situation. I needed a strategy. I needed to think on my feet—because selling printing jobs to walk-in clients wasn't going to cut it. I'd spend an hour with someone who needed business cards, giving them all I could and more, and the company would make twenty bucks.

I was used to closing fifty-thousand-dollar deals. This approach wouldn't get me or Connect to the goals I was outlining. The store needed more, and I knew I could get more.

After learning that I left Interlude, word got around pretty quickly. My absence had created a gap of sorts. One day, I got a call from one of their Regionals. She was struggling and needed some ideas.

I knew she had a large marketing budget, and I was trying to build this business for Connect in the printing industry with no experience. So, I came up with a solution.

"I realize you'd catch heat if you hired a consultant," I told her over the phone, "but if you spend your marketing budget with me, I'll fly out and consult for free."

I figured, what the heck? All she could do is say no—and then I'd just be in the same place I already was.

To my surprise, I heard a single word come through the phone line: "Done." Griffey had just made another play, and my new career was about to take a major leap.

I drove out to a small random town down in inland Southern California, some dot on a map. I got down there and toured the location. Right away, I discovered some issues with their processes. They were giving tours like they were selling fast food, with the mentality to offer the product, whether it is bought or not. They were investing no time in making connections to their leads, taking no time to get to know them—not to mention there seemed to be zero consistency in their marketing approach.

My lens was telling me that they should be developing a tour route, one that included a discovery room where they could sit and get to know the clients, where they could sit and show some compassion in their approach. Plus, I felt, they needed to establish a marketing plan to align advertising and event promotions.

I created a plan. In essence, I customized a playbook for their locations that gave simple steps to tour and close—and when and where the advertisements should go in order to generate leads.

I also designed a unique direct mail program to grow the building's census. A hybrid of the Playbook, tailored to this specific locations needs. The industry had been targeting entire areas, which I found too broad of a stroke. We needed to achieve greater accuracy, pinpoint our efforts, and be sharper.

To achieve this, I reviewed data points from the entire last year of move-ins. From my research, I was able to identify a core audience, those we needed to target. I got the system up and running and generated lists that fit the company's ideal client. I designed a no nonsense postcard that asked, in specific terms, what we wanted from the lead, and sent them out. Lead-generation boomed.

I've since used this tactic with several other companies and made them millions of dollars.

Handily, this one location's budget for direct mail was equivalent to a week's worth of work printing at Connect from their current walk-in clients. I made the revenue of a week in a single day! Better yet, I figured out a way to make this order happen monthly with only about an hour more of work every thirty days. I built the process, made it extremely efficient and it just started running on autopilot.

I knew I was onto something, something big. I was done taking walk-in orders for twenty bucks a pop.

I fixed that one Interlude location and, as a result, they wanted me to fix another. Then another. Then another.

As my program took off and started generating consistent leads, Interlude came to me and wanted my program implemented at all their properties. They were essentially acquiring, through me, an extra Managing Director to solve their problems for free: they only paid me for something they were going to spend money on anyway.

Contrary to the Law of Conservation of Energy, my new strategy was seemingly making something out of nothing. It was a big gold nugget just sitting in the creek and waiting to be picked up.

My consulting career was now in full swing.

Region after region signed on with me. Within six months of joining Connect, I'd already grown the printing business to their prior year's annual revenue.

After seeing what I was doing, the owner signed a deal with me to make us 50/50 business partners. It felt great. I had made a big play—I finally found a way to earn the amount of money I wanted while also having the ability to control my schedule. It felt even better than any island in that sea of bad I was used to; I felt like I was finally navigating out into healthy, wide-open waters.

Things started well and then got better. I grew Connect year over year by over 100 percent, turning a three hundred thousand dollar-a-year business into a multi-million-dollar business in a little over two years.

No more mowing lawns. No more struggling to keep the pantry full. My consulting work combined with my customized direct mail program equaled money for everyone. Even me.

SPA DAY

The more I advanced in my career, the more money I made, sure, but at the same time, it continued to feel like it was not enough.

I was definitely moving the needle. For the first time in my life, I had some extra, a surplus, money that was not going straight to bills and necessities.

Jill and I saved up and we went to Hawaii for our anniversary! We got out there and the beaches were white, the water was teal, and the sunsets were fire. It was paradise. Our hotel was right on the beach and the island culture was just so good. It was all alohas and mahalos from sunrise to lights out.

And the hotel had a spa. A nice one. I'd never seen anything like it outside of a movie. I looked up the prices. Not cheap, but, I thought to myself, *my Jill deserves this.*

I booked two full-day packages and spent a thousand percent increase on what a box of animal crackers was going to cost me. So what? That day, Jill and I were going to celebrate us.

When that spa opened in the morning, I made sure we were the first people in there. I was going to get our money's worth. I was going to maximize the cost versus value.

Almost everything was open-air right out to the beach. Jill and I were professionally relaxed and pampered all day, enjoying the sounds of the rolling waves behind us while receiving our first ever professional massages. Open-air showers were made from lava rock, fresh fruit and drinks were served straight from the island, and the feeling of easy, leisurely luxury was amazing.

Lunch was delivered right by the pool, and we enjoyed the meal with the sounds of waves crashing around us.

As the sun descended in the west, Jill and I headed to our separate locker rooms. I took one last trip to the sauna and then showered off.

On my way back to the lockers, at the white countertops, I found myself astounded: there was all this stuff, bath products that you are encouraged to take along with you, like full bottles of shampoo and brand-new little combs and razors. Free stuff, there for you to just take with you.

A few of these bottles were coming home with me. *You know that's right!*

I grabbed a few, but not a ton by any means. I was feeling all happy, but as I walked back to my locker, a couple of older guys looked at me, eyeing me with their chuckles like I was just the young kid who needed the free samples and didn't really "belong."

They continued to mock me, talking to one another as if I wasn't there. I tried to ignore it, but their body language and micro-expressions were just oozing with disgust.

They continued to push it. They made comments like "looks like they're letting just anyone in now" and "I didn't realize this resort was getting so cheap. I guess it's time to find a new place to go." To which they each laughed loudly.

I felt small.

It got under my skin in a big way, them throwing their judgment on me, deciding for me if I belonged or not.

This is part of the lie. The judgment that follows is to keep those that "don't belong" out of the inner circle. I am telling you that you don't have to play this rigged game. You can choose if you want to be here or not, unfortunately I didn't understand this yet.

So, without saying anything, I tucked my head and threw my stuff in my bag. I got out of the spa area as quickly as I could. I met up with Jill and we walked to the car, all the while I was still holding onto the embarrassment. I just couldn't shake it.

As I started driving, Jill said, so lovingly, "That was just about the most amazing day I've ever had." Then she looked out to the water and sighed.

"What a once-in-a-lifetime opportunity."

I couldn't take it anymore and pulled over to the side of the road. Jill could tell I was upset.

"What's wrong?" she asked.

I told her about what happened and how this is *not* going to be "a once in a lifetime thing." I explained that she deserved to have this every day if she wanted. I truly meant it.

In this moment, I tell my wife that this will *not* be the greatest day of her life. I tell her how not long ago, something as small as buying animal crackers felt impossible. I tell her that spa days and unbelievable trips are going to be a normal thing in our lives.

And the only way I saw to make it all come true was to make more money. The only way I knew how to make more money was to work harder, so that's what I did. And as you'll see down the line, it was taking its toll on my body and my family.

Part of the lie, part of the rigged game's rulebook is to keep us spending darn near all the money that comes in, no matter how much money starts coming in. This keeps us working hard, always escalating, which ultimately is not good for us. For our mind and our bodies.

In life, regardless of who you are, the world will come at you to tear you down. This will happen, but how you handle it will dictate your results. As you've already read and will continue to read, I am a positive person. This isn't just a bland statement I drop, but a reflection of how I live my life. It's in my actions every single day.

As the world comes for you, choose to use this to your advantage. For me, facing the people that thought I wasn't worth the time of day gave fuel to my fire. It burned my desire to continue to prove them wrong, to prove my generational cycle wrong, to prove I was worth something. You might not feel this way today, or tomorrow, but if you keep putting in the work, choosing to pursue what makes you happy, and facing adversity with a positive mind, I promise you that you won't be lost out to sea.

MIND & BODY

As the money increased, so did my appetite. I wanted more money, and on top of it, I wanted more food. Without sound health-bearing and having the money to get all the groceries I wanted, I ate more and more. I started to gain weight. A lot of it.

Because of my dad and how my overall family life was growing up, drinking a ton never really appealed to me. Eating became my way to cope. Fast food was my go-to, alongside anything sweet. I could eat macarons like no one's business!

As Connect grew, I was back to traveling and honestly my eating habits were anything but healthy. I was inconsistent, filled with fast food options, and ate in extremely large quantities.

I never once considered the impact this unhealthy approach could cause in my life. What I was subjecting my body to was not sustainable. I had no idea that there would be another obstacle in finding my success, especially one that involved my weight.

One morning, I stepped on the scale. I almost couldn't read it for two reasons—my giant belly and the fact that I'd literally almost gone off the scales.

When I finally saw the number, it read 332 lbs.

Without realizing it, I was pushing myself so hard, not taking the breaks for sleep, to eat appropriately, to exercise. All of my time went to working hard, learning more, and advancing myself.

I looked in the mirror and just couldn't take it any longer. I was tired of seeing myself this way. I knew this would cost me if I kept this pace up. I wanted more for myself and my family. So, I made a change. I was an athlete when I was younger, and I could be again.

I started working out. Hard. Twice a day, like "double days" from fall football camp. I bought the Insanity program from Beachbody. The trainer on the TV, Shaun T, became my best friend.

I cut my calorie intake by fifteen hundred a day, and I went from eating fast food and ice cream sundaes to salads, salmon, and shakes.

I knew I had to change myself. I didn't accept fate, I instead went about doing what I could do to change my future, so I went to work. I started training, started eating right, and started making a difference in my life. I trained my body by practicing martial arts, doing CrossFit, and playing sports whenever possible. I even trained for, and competed in a couple of Tough Mudder events, something I never thought would be possible.

Losing over 100 lbs was a course correction in my navigation. I'm now at a healthy (and even fairly athletic) 220 lbs.

And there's no way I could've done it without Jill's help. She's been there for me and with me every step of the way.

I knew there was the option of just stopping, not working hard, and not being diligent about maintaining the changes I'd implemented. It wasn't easy to give up the bad eating habits. Working out was not always what I wanted to be doing, but I knew I *had* to.

I felt I needed to push, and push beyond, without concern for my own well-being. This was what the world told me was the way to find success, the only way to play. To always go all out.

Balance in your life does require health. Look, I'm not here for a fitness lecture or even a full section on how to eat better. I just want you to stop and think about your health for just a moment. Your body needs to balance with your mind. Like most books, this is here to strengthen your mind, but please don't forget to do something about the body. I was so focused that I lost sight of this fact and it cost me way more than I thought it ever could.

Take the time to evaluate your body, find a routine that works for you, and if you find something is off like I did. Don't wait, get help, and get your body aligned so it can keep up with you on your path to find YOUR SUCCESS.

We live in a society that still largely admires the act of "grinding." This is part of the lie, and the rigged game I keep talking about. The perception that "to grind" is good is one of the rules that helps the rigged game remain rigged. There are lies in this approach, dangers that are not discussed.

"Grinding" typically coincides with bad eating habits and even worse sleeping habits. These bad habits seem to go hand in hand when pushing beyond your limits.

I continued growing Connect and really didn't do it with much balance. Before we knew it, Connect was now consulting in over seventy properties for Interlude. Trouble was, I was the only consultant at Connect.

There was never enough time. I needed to find ways to cut corners and save some time. With my body back where it needed to be, I felt like I could push even harder. Sure, I was eating better and exercising, but I wasn't yet strong enough to set the boundaries I needed to with my work-life balance. So the unhealthy habits returned.

Consulting for so many properties brought me back to a life of travel and late nights. I returned to putting myself through nights of only two to four hours of sleep. I was healthier, so I felt I could take it, but I wasn't listening to what my body needed.

I was 29. I had come a long way from sleeping behind a futon, but I was still blind to a lot. I felt I needed to push further.

I found myself using the unhealthy habits I was forced to endure at Interlude. But now, I was choosing to do this to myself. At Interlude, My body was force-trained for this, and I was now good at it. I could skip food, sleep, personal time, anything. I could cut it all out to drive more toward more "success".

As Connect removed the cellular avenues to focus on printing and consulting, I keep pushing to take on more consulting gigs.

It wasn't too uncommon for my business partner and I to each put in two sleepless nights a week to accomplish what we were building together. Our bond grew deep—working side-by-side, making money, pushing our skills to the limits, and finding a new way to expand upon them.

But this approach was costing me more than I knew. I was working toward what I felt was the right path, but I wasn't quite getting there the right way yet.

I felt like I was attaining the success that I was told I was supposed to want. I was on top of my game. Consulting on a higher level than I'd yet to do in my career to this point. I had all the right answers, I was solving all the problems, I was generating millions of dollars in revenue for my clients and for Connect.

I truly felt like nothing could stop me. But the grind caught up with me. In a big way.

Part Eight

"There's a million things I haven't done. Just you wait, just you wait."

- Lin-Manuel Miranda, Hamilton

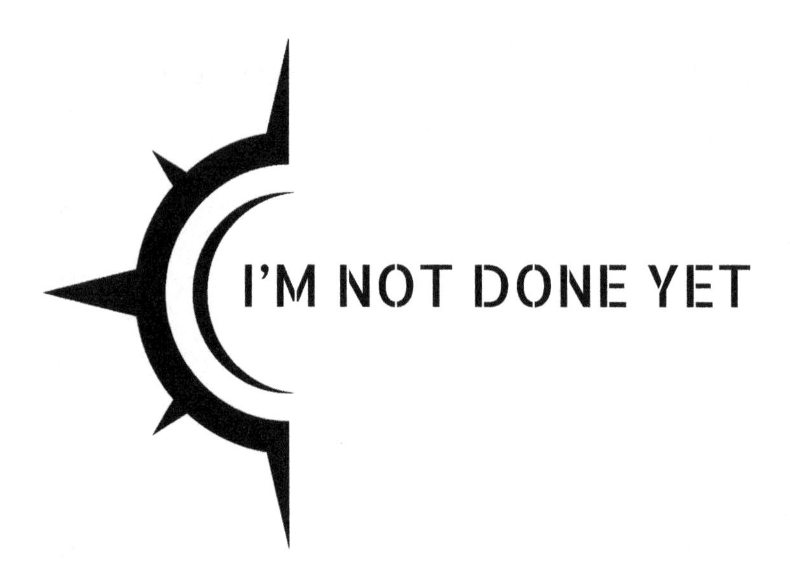

I'M NOT DONE YET

I got a day off from the chaos of work, and Jill and I were at home watching movies. Ren was with her grandparents, and Jill and I were enjoying a relaxing day getting some laughs out of an Adam Sandler movie. I was calm, not thinking much beyond the humor Sandler offers when I felt a *pop*.

It didn't hurt. There was no pain. Just a pop and a strange sensation within the center of my chest. It sent an odd feeling through my soul, but I tried to ignore it.

Instantly, Jill knew something was wrong. "What is it?" she asked.

"I felt a pop… in my chest… kinda like bubble wrap…"

"That's odd…" She said, her voice full of concern.

"I'm fine," I told her, "let's just watch the movie."

After a few minutes, however, I started to get extremely uncomfortable—still no pain, but now my shirt was feeling tight. I looked down at my chest; it was starting to swell; I knew something is seriously wrong.

We dashed to the car and jumped in, but we don't really know where to go. I called my doctor, he said to come to see him. He's about an hour's drive away.

Halfway there, I felt a second *pop*.

This one was worse. Much worse. Excruciating pain began setting in and I could feel my body start filling with blood. I knew that I was dying.

Then, I blacked out. My head hit the window and I woke up however long later to Jill screaming at me to stay awake. I did. I fought back and managed to keep my eyes open. We both knew that if I fell asleep, I would never wake up again.

Jill began intentionally prodding me to stay awake, almost nagging at me as she poked emotional buttons so I don't fall back asleep. Her tactics worked, and I didn't black out again throughout the rest of the ride.

Jill's heroics in driving and keeping me awake finally led to us arriving at the hospital to meet my doctor. I arrived, and it became obvious that I needed to get into a room quickly. If I didn't get into surgery, I'd be dead within the hour.

But they were completely full. I thought back to my father, my life flashing before my eyes in waves of images.

My doctor hurried into the exam room and looked me in the eye.

"I'm not letting you die, Billy. I'm cutting you open right here and now. Jill, you should leave. This is going to get messy."

Jill refused to leave my side. He didn't even have all the proper tools, but I knew we were doing this.

"Take a breath and then don't move," he told me severely, "or I may accidentally kill you."

As I saw him approach me with his knife, I felt the fear rising. I convinced myself that I needed to stay alive for Ren and Jill.

With my shirt raised, the doctor brought the scalpel to my chest. Then, like out of a movie, just before he makes his first incision, a nurse burst into the waiting room. "We got a room!!" she yelled.

I'm prepped for surgery in a matter of minutes. Blood was filling up my chest, I could feel it. As I lay down on the table, I could not see over my swollen chest and belly. I looked at Jill and we both knew this may very well be the last time we see each other on this side. We were stunned and unsure of what to say.

"I love you, my Jill," I whispered to her as they started to wheel me away.

"You better come back to me," she replied through tears.

As I'm about to be put under, I looked around and noticed the looks in the eyes of the doctor and nurses. They were full of concern. I was overwhelmed with the awareness that this may be my last conscious thought as Billy Thompson. I had only one thought running through my mind: that no one was going to explain this properly to my daughter.

In that potentially final moment, I realized that she wasn't ready to not have her dad. I wasn't ready at 16, and at 7, I know Ren is not either. She needs me.

Right before they put me under, I said four words: "I'm not done yet."

As they counted down from ten, I didn't know if I would ever wake up.

And then, I died.

My heart stopped. I'm still not sure for how long, but I know that it happened. The pop in my chest turned out to be an 'arterial burst' that caused me to lose two-thirds of my blood internally.

On that table, after they put me under, I was cut in half so the docs could find the burst. They worked for hours on me - me dying somewhere during that time - but they brought me back from the other side, resuscitated me, and stitched me back together.

The doctor went out to talk with Jill.

"He had an arterial aneurysm rupture."

Later we found out this has less than a 1% survival rate.

Sometimes, I suppose, a fraction of a percent is all you need.

LUMEGENT IS BORN

They can only speculate on what happened to me during that time. I was only 30; someone as young and seemingly healthy as me should have never faced such a rare condition. My doctors explained, obviously so, that it was most likely caused by the stress and pressures I'd been putting my body through for so long.

Damn the grind.

Learn from me: don't kill yourself for your work. All the money, recognition, or status in the world ain't worth crap if you're dead. No matter how much wealth we attain in our lives, we're all the same corpses when we're dead. Stick around for your family and yourself.

What I can say about dying is that it recalibrates your mind, how you see things, and what you value. The stresses of the world don't seem to matter nearly as much anymore. Though I was bedridden for months after the event due to the lasting effects of the massive blood loss.

I didn't know this at the time, but the owners of Connect were feeling the effects of burnout too. After a couple of months of recovery, it became obvious that some things needed to change.

When I got back on my feet, we agreed to part ways; Connect would stay on and help Northern Nevada with a new, local printing business. After almost seeing heaven, I knew I had to expand my reach—and so I went global.

I could no longer sit back and not be and do all that I was meant to be and do. The fact that death comes to us all was now more apparent in my mind's eye than ever before. How I had been so blind to it before those pops in my chest, I do not know. I no longer feared death; all I feared was not using my life to find and be what I was looking for. I wasn't going to leaving my Jill and Ren with nothing. I needed to build more for them, and quickly.

I felt the clock. I could feel that my life wasn't going to be as long as most; like it was pulled directly out of a musical: "Lately, I've Been Hearing This Sound Everywhere I Go. Like a Tick, Tick, Tick." The writer of *Tick, Tick, Boom* was a man named Mr. Jonathan Larson. After working for the better part of a decade on the musical, *Rent!*, Larson died, suddenly and unexpectedly, the day before his play opened for the first of what would become a twelve-year sold-out run. Mr. Larson died young from the same medical condition that almost killed me.

Carpe Diem. Don't wait—Do. Things. Now.

I'd always felt like my time was going to be short in my life. Maybe it was growing up seeing my dad's life being cut short. I don't know. My time is running out, I can hear the clock ticking and I must find my success before I go, I must.

But I do know that when I left Connect to start Lumegent, for the first time the business was solely mine. I was finally at the helm of my own ship. No more seeking out islands in seas of bad. I was going to go on a cruise into teal waters and endless skies. I felt free, just me, charting my own course. I wanted to rebuild everything.

Nothing could stop me.

Starting Lumegent was when I truly started doing success my way. I started my consulting firm with a unique, vintage approach to business. I wanted a modern business model in the mentalities of old.

Lumegent began with a unique, vintage approach to business. Establishing partnerships with our clients. Deep, lasting, connecting relationships to work together as a team. We entered the consulting space once more but also continued with our expertise in printing.

I came to feel that the best way to defy the lie, to beat the rigged game, was to go forward by going backward. Unlike what I had experienced previously, my focus now would not be to reap as much profit as I could generate but to sow my fields toward goals of longevity. I would make the most out of what I had so I could ensure a long-term, sustainable company.

That's why I established Lumegent as a C-Corp: I would reinvest in the business, making larger percentages of funding proportionately available to my employees, and to pillar-type infrastructures based around the people-centric business. In addition, I would give back to the communities in which I lived, worked, and depended. Charities would get their time, energy, and resources just like revenue reports got. We would be balanced.

I began by defining our culture and our mission. Only then would we start to do business. I resolved that, when we grew, we would grow with balance. Human beings would be treated as human beings, not as cogs for increased revenue. From the start, we offered full health insurance benefits, even to spouses and dependents. I'd seen a lack of insurance too much in my life and I was tired of it. A 401k at a six percent match with a bonus program set by each employee was a given, and schedule flexibility opportunities were a must.

I knew that if I gave employees back control of their lives, they would be happier and more fulfilled. With that give, I knew there would be a symbiotic give on the other end because that's how the universe works. I mean, this is why the four-day working week is a growing trend.

When the culture and mission were in place, I did an internal review and found that 70 percent of our revenue was being generated by two percent of our clients. So, my first decision was obvious: to cut 98 percent of our client base.

Sure, it was risky. But I knew that if we could pull it off we would allow the team to focus on what was working, giving our energy toward what was most important. Because, what we feed, grows.

This refocus would allow us to take on additional clients - geared toward what we'd learned about our *ideal* ones - without needing to hire more staff. This refocusing, this new lens - along with fulfilled employees - allowed us to work incredibly efficiently. Less can be more, and we hoped to show that.

As expected, revenue initially dropped but the numbers recovered quickly. I remember watching the film *Jerry McGuire* around that time. If you haven't seen it, it's the Tom Cruise-led story of a hotshot sports agent who loses all but one client after his from-the-heart "mission statement" is read by his firm's c-suite.

The story - loosely based upon the iconic Leigh Steinburg - shows a guy building his business back on his *own* terms, built through human connection, inspiration, and the knowledge that "the human head weighs eight pounds."

Lumegent focused on our best clients; we gave them our energy so it could be exchanged elsewhere. Within a few weeks, we transitioned our clients to other vendors. We provided contacts to other printers in the area that were willing to take on the clients, including sending many over to a new local start-up. This opened up the capacity to take on new leads, clients we would have otherwise had to turn down due to capacity limits.

The door was definitely opening. Then, a gust picked up and the thing flung wide open.

I'd supported a Regional with Interlude through acquisitions and, one day, out of the clear blue sky, Olivia reached out to me. She was now running a company we'll call Mason Services, they were one of the largest in the death services industry, and she needed my help. My help, with a two million dollar printing budget.

In exchange, she asked for what I've always given: free consulting, but the right to handle the print.

We were all but ready to push play, but she offered one little stipulation: "You'll have to be in Philadelphia by Monday morning."

It was 6 pm on Saturday evening.

"Sure thing, no problem."

I booked the first flight on Sunday morning. Reno to Denver, and on to Philly. It's winter, but I thought we'd be okay.

Nope.

I woke up the next morning and checked my phone: ice storm. Jets are freezing left and right and only a handful are getting out. Not mine. Jill performed a little magic and got me a seat on the only flight to still set to depart. Up to Seattle.

She drove me to the airport and off I went. But, up in Sea-Tac, my flight to Philly was canceled. No problem, I booked a standby that took me to Denver. At least I was finally heading east.

I descended over the Rockies and landed at Denver International. I was making progress. What wasn't good was when I looked up to the departure board and saw that all eastbound flights had just been grounded. My heart sank. What the heck was I gonna do?

I got back on the phone with Jill again and miraculously, she found a new option. It was the only way, but not without its risk. I took a new flight path that sent me back down to Phoenix. I'd fly southwest, then on to Chicago where I could catch the last flight of the day up to Philadelphia.

I made it down to Arizona but things with takeoff and landing up to Chicago didn't go as efficiently as I would have liked. I landed at O'Hare and only had 16 minutes to get from Terminal 1 to Terminal 3 (if you've ever been there, you know that's not an easy task).

My head was dripping with sweat, and I was out of breath, feeling the opportunity slipping through my fingers. If I failed to catch this plane, I would not be there on time on Monday morning. Even if I rented a car and drove through the night, I wouldn't make it there in time for that meeting. The largest single deal I've ever closed was about to collapse, all because of snow and ice.

I only had my backpack and my briefcase, but they felt like they weighed a hundred pounds as I ran as fast as I could, yelling out, "Pleeeaaase… hold that flight!"

They did. Just for a minute, but that's all I needed. I finally got to my seat, dripping in sweat and feeling sorry for the guy next to me.

I remained on alert the whole flight, my anxiety convincing me that I wasn't out of the troubled waters just yet. The puddle jump over to Philly went off without too many hitches, but I wasn't done yet. By the time I landed, it was well past midnight. The rental car place wouldn't be open for much longer. I awkwardly sprinted to the rental place, a lopsided run as my briefcase bashed against my legs. I finally arrived in a heap of sweat and secured just about the last car in the place - an overpriced luxury Chrysler - but I didn't care.

I opened up the door and took my seat behind the wheel to embark on the hour-plus drive on frozen backroads up to a tiny little town in the middle of nowhere.

The car wouldn't start. "Are you serious!" I cried out loud—I've been renting cars almost every week for years, and not once has this happened to me.

I rushed out and went back to the guy at the counter, asking for anything. I'd take a bike at this point.

An hour later, they found another car: A tiny compact Ford.

I hit the road. I managed to not skid out too often and made it to my hotel a little after 2 am, somehow in one piece.

By this time, the meeting was scheduled to start in five hours. I hadn't eaten anything but peanuts. No problem. There was a Wawa - the single greatest market on the planet - right next door to my hotel. After a day of battling the weather, I cannot tell you what a godsend this was. I scarfed down a meatball grinder and some TastyKakes (delicious) and managed to get to bed by 3:30, knowing full well that the next day was the first day of the rest of my life.

I woke up and made it over to the 7 am meeting on time. Right away, I knew I was in the big leagues. The company was much larger than I expected and if I wanted to land the initial two million dollar budget, I needed to help Olivia rebuild her entire marketing team to make it run more efficiently.

"Sure thing," I said, knowing full well I was not backing down on my chance for a starting spot in the Major Leagues.

Olivia then walked me over to a conference room where the entire department is waiting. She introduced me to the team and let them know that I would be interviewing every employee in marketing and sales. I was to be tasked with some final decisions and I would rebuild the department from within. I would then work with this new team to build out the new marketing and advertising strategies for the organization.

Olivia walked me into the room, looked at me, and calmly said, "Okay, Billy, they're all yours," and then she walked out of the room.

I was 31 years old and had just been handed the keys to drive marketing for a half billion dollar a year company.

Then, it happened—life, like it does, repeated itself.

One of the longtime employees spoke up, cutting the silence in the room. "Yeah, I've been here for over twenty years and you're some kid. Why are we expected to listen to you?"

And so, I said the line again: "Because I'm the person who decides if you have a job at the end of the day, that's why."

Only, this time I said it with more of a smile. It worked, I gained control of the room. It was a bold start, but a necessary one.

"Let's get to work," I said.

NEW HEIGHTS

During the first month of Lumegent's operations, we had already gained new million dollar clients and begun conversations with even more big players. With my deep understanding of the senior living industry, death services made a lot of sense. I came to realize that all of the experiences throughout my life that I've told you about, all the details of my career, had all led me here. I felt like there wasn't one problem I couldn't solve, no situation I was scared to face. Everything made sense. I wore a lot of hats and worked with a lot of employees on a lot of levels, and in less than a month, I'd rebuilt the marketing department at Mason Services, and grew Lumegent to a team of 20.

During the rebuilding process of Mason Services, I kept things simple. The people who were motivated and wanted to be on the team stayed on. Before I got there, it felt like the company was built on tenure. I didn't care about tenure. Didn't play the politics either. I wanted effort, dedication, and skillsets. I looked specifically for these traits because those are the building blocks of great teams. And business - even for the solo entrepreneur - is about the team.

I was simultaneously building the culture and techniques at Mason Services while flying home to do the same with the Lumegent team.I was building two marketing organizations congruently. It felt great. Life was changing.

As Lumegent began to take shape, life at home was also changing. One of those changes came about when my little sister, Samantha (Sami), came back into my life. Mom moved to be closer to us and it didn't take long for Samantha to become reconnected with us. After a few months, she was a constant feature at Jill's side. When I came home from trips, she'd be at my house. If we went anywhere, she was with us. Then she was with us all the time. In short, Samantha became part of our family.

Soon enough, Ren and Sami became like sisters. Our family was growing right alongside our business. Sami filled a space we didn't know we were missing. Our family was now complete. Our bond grew deeper and deeper, day after day. Jill and I now had another daughter, Ren had a sister, and we all couldn't be happier.

Even as everything changed around me, I remained driven. For all I've told you about those things from the sea of bad, I had this perpetual chip on my shoulder. I tried not to wear it, but it was there—telling me how I wasn't "worthy" of being successful.

I needed to prove that the rigged game could be beaten, that what I had always been told about what my life would be was a lie. That I could build something for my family.

I felt like I was doing it. Even if just a little bit, because I felt, I knew, that I was beating it myself, and, I knew that if I could rewrite my rulebook, anyone could.

At Mason Services, my team started a social media campaign that was getting results, and after not too long we were given the opportunity to rebrand the entire corporation. A corporation of immense size was trusting a small fish like Lumegent to rebrand them. New logos, new content strategy, new branding, new taglines, new sales and marketing strategies; site visit training, executive coaching, motivational speaking… the works.

And everything - all the revenue, all the product launches, all the devlopment - started with the building of relationships. It started with trust.

My theory that Lumegent could work together with organizations as a true team as opposed to a standard vendor/client agreement was proving true. No hierarchies. No politics, just: how do we all work optimally together so we can achieve the most?

Our team was *their* team and we all trusted each other. That's why Lumegent and Mason Services did so many great things together.

After a while, Olivia deemed that I'd successfully rebuilt the marketing department, and I gained the two million dollar budget. It was like all of a sudden being able to fly. We further redeveloped programs and processes and when we fully took over social media, we brought in another couple of million.

It was your to-the-moon, overnight success. And I'll take it.

Lumegent expanded quickly to keep up with all of our new clients. Like we'd done with Interlude, we were building direct mail and marketing strategies, handling printing, and fixing issues. Everything was moving so quickly we just couldn't train new consultants fast enough, so I had no choice but to fly back and forth to each client.

The grind was creeping back in but at the pace we were growing, it was hard to see.

My travel went from three days a week to four. It was déjà vu. I wanted to set boundaries, but they kept getting pushed out. Before long, I would be out of town for weeks at a time.

I was traveling all over the world for work. We would help a client in Philly, then head up to Canada, bounce to a client in Spain, and then over to Puerto Rico and back home for a visit in California. It was madness.

I found myself missing Sami's choir concerts. I wasn't there after school to help Ren with her homework. Jill and I were losing touch. Things were changing, constantly, too quickly for me to keep up with.

I was building this amazing company, but something felt wrong.

THE END OF SOMEONE ELSE'S SUCCESS

Shortly after getting back from a whirlwind of business in Puerto Rico, I was already way up in Toronto, Canada. I spent the day picking out my new office for Lumegent in a building that looked over what is considered the Wall Street of the city. It was a beautiful top floor office with glass walls. I could see the entire city. It was gorgeous.

Outwardly, things were beyond going well. Lumegent was growing by leaps and bounds and the money was coming in.

But I was breaking promises again—promises to myself and promises to my family. Something wasn't right. I couldn't count the number of times I'd made the commitment to work less, to travel less, but I still went and did it. It's just that to build up success in this rigged game, I would have to spend my time away from home. Away from my girls.

The grind was returning, back to the time when I almost lost my life (I know, I thought I was past this too). I was gone, not sleeping, not eating healthily, not working out, and not with my girls. I thought I was following my own course, but I was still playing this rigged game, following their course.

I felt true in my conviction that I had to do this. But I was burning out. Again.

My time was almost cut short by my own body and its reaction to the grind, which led me to the feeling that I still wouldn't have much time left, so I needed to build the money, a legacy… something to leave my girls. Sitting in that office in Toronto, absorbing the breathtaking view, I should have thought I was the most successful I had ever been. I should have been happy.

I wasn't.

I was about to step into a level of success I'd never dreamed of, yet what I was feeling was not success. I felt like I was failing. Like what I was earning meant nothing. Why?

Then it hit me. The cost and the value just didn't make sense. I was in a position that would be considered successful but I just felt alone. I wasn't at home with my daughters, Ren and Sami, nor having any time with my Jill.

No value will ever be worth the cost of my family. So why would I choose to be away from them again? This might be someone's success, but it was not MY SUCCESS.

I would have to make a change, firmly, and for the final time. But I felt trapped. I was stuck in the lie, bound to play the rigged game. How could I take care of my family if I walked away from this? What would I be able to leave them?

These fears filled me, I felt split in two. One side wanted to be home, the other wanted to provide. Why couldn't I have both?

If we landed this opportunity, Lumegent would triple in size. The potential client in Toronto was a big player. The owner was excited to work with me. She wanted me to rebrand her corporation in the vein of what I'd done for Mason Services. My unique approach had somehow reached her, and she wanted me to do the same for her. I knew I could do what she wanted me to do. I knew Lumegent could and would hit it out of the park. All I had to do was show up, have dinner, and sign the deal.

This one deal would put our company's value at over a hundred million dollars.

Easy choice, right?

I got to my hotel room, checked my dry cleaning to ensure my suit had been pressed, and laid it out for the dinner meeting. I walked over to the window and looked down on the lights of the city from my penthouse suite. I was on top of the world and should have felt as such.

But again, I felt empty. I felt alone.

So, I called my Jill.

"Hey, pal," I said heavily.

"Hey, how'd the meeting go?" she asked.

"The first one's done. All I have to do is go to dinner and sign the contract."

She told me that she was proud of me.

"Yeah…," I managed, wanting to say more. She picked up the hesitation in my voice, sensing that there was something I wasn't saying.

"What's wrong?" she asked. "Isn't this what you want?"

Knowing the timeline from my last rebrand, I told her that if I took the new project, it would take me at least three years to accomplish it.

"Isn't this what you want?" she asked again.

My head was filled with fog, a blur of all the time that had passed and all the time that would pass if I took this career-defining project. It hadn't even been a full two years, and we'd already reached this level of success. But it wasn't right. I didn't feel successful.

"What I want," I told my wife, "is to drop everything. I just want to drive to the airport and come home and never look back."

"Then why don't you?" she asked pointedly.

"What?" I said, with incredulity.

"Why don't you just come home?"

I asked her if she truly comprehended what I was saying. I told her that I was talking about walking away from the company, throwing away millions of dollars. Not to sell the company, mind you, but to just walk away from it all and come home. If I were to sell, the process would take at least a year. I wanted my life to start now.

"I know how you feel, because I feel the same. We don't need all of this, we just need you. It's always been enough for us just to be together. We will figure it out," my Jill said. "So do it, come home."

Her words were like the warmest blanket on the coldest night. Her words told me, once and for all, that she didn't want the fame, the money, the status—just me.

For the first time in my life I could clearly see. It wasn't about building more and more. It wasn't about creating something to leave behind. I finally understood, it was about my life, right now.

I looked out that penthouse window once more, looked out into the cityscape, and thought about the trajectory of my life. I thought about MY SUCCESS. My resolve was absolute: I cancelled the meeting, packed my bags, and headed home.

I was no longer going to follow the lie, I threw away the rigged game's version of success to chart my own course. To be home.

With my girls.

Over the next few months back home, I closed out Lumegent's client contracts. I explained the decision to close to my team in a way they could understand, as a failure. The organization would no longer be able to operate as it once was. I knew that few of my team members if any, would understand what I was about to do.

But I was not in it for my ego—I was finally ready to say goodbye and chart my course to find MY SUCCESS.

I transitioned my staff to new jobs in the community. I gave away my book of business and sold our ten thousand-square-foot building. I sold our two million dollars worth of equipment for pennies on the dollar. I packed up only a studio-office worth of materials and said goodbye to the old Lumegent.

There were no tears, no pain, no remorse—because the cost of the company had come to outweigh its value. My life, my health, and my girls far outweighed the company I'd built. I wasn't going to waste another moment chasing a success that wasn't my own.

I had the recipe. If I needed to make something again, I knew I could just go out and do it. On my terms.

I walked away from millions of dollars. I closed up shop on the old Lumegent. I came home. I spent time with my girls. I relaxed and breathed and lived in the moment. I came to celebrate the little things, realizing that they were, indeed, the big things.

And then, when the time was right, I started the new Lumegent. The only thing that was the same was the name. My Jill had come up with the name - it means "bringing light to mind"- and together we set out to create something truly special.

I set out to sea, this time fearless of the open waters. I knew where my safe islands were (my home, my girls) and I was going to set a course that would always keep those islands close to me.

This would provide me with the life I wanted. I ignored what the world told me was standard and built a plan for my work and my company that fit my lifestyle, not the typical endless hours of grinding I'd done my entire career.

I decided that Lumegent would operate with a business plan that could be kept to a small team, with low overheads and strong vendor relationships.

Without needing a full executive team, I could manage the entire process, and one of my first decisions was to make Lumegent a consulting agency that could choose the clients I wanted to work with and decline anyone I didn't.

I didn't feel like I would be chasing money anymore as I'd always done, but rather let it come to me. I didn't always have to say "yes." If a client wouldn't respect my time (personally and professionally), I wouldn't bring them on. Or if a project would exceed too many hours and affect my time at home, I would simply say no. I did all of this because I finally understood the cost and value of money and time in my life.

I would make Lumegent the way I wanted, the way that worked for my path and not simply the way I was "supposed" to. I knew my value, and so, I finally committed to only working with those who also knew this value. I would help people the way I wanted. I would rebrand—speak, give lectures, teach, train. Whatever I felt I could do to bring a positive change to people's lives. No boxes, no cages, just me fluidly and abundantly doing what I could to help.

This is the new Lumegent.

MY SUCCESS

In our lives, we are all faced with decisions to be made and outcomes to be had. We win some, we lose some. But not all games are as black and white as the numbers on a scoreboard at the end of a baseball game. Losses can, and often do, come with upsides. That's why, rather than looking at things as utter failures or unflinching successes, I encourage people to look at the *cost versus value* of the situation. Especially, the ones in which you've failed—because you haven't.

The trouble is, we tend to look at failure as a pain point, a sharp pain to avoid at all costs—and then, when it comes, to ignore it, to not think about it.

I say, don't do this. I say look at your "failures" and analyze them. Learn from your mistakes.

And know that mistakes aren't always mistakes. Sometimes a sidestep or even a backward step gets you where you are going better than going straight forward. Avoid looking at the failure as something bad or wrong, but rather as a moment to compare cost versus value.

The value in failure lay in the missed opportunities that straightforward success robs you of. Yeah, maybe you're getting good money to keep doing what you are doing, but you are *still* doing what you've been doing. Change can be good, and the beauty of failure is how it often gives us the excuse to do something new—sometimes even, that thing you've always wanted to do.

That was how it was with me.

During the time old Lumegent was a twenty million dollar company, I made a big mistake. I made an extremely poor choices in hiring some of my executive team. The situation started rough and got progressively worse.

It felt like they were attempting to destroy everything I had worked so hard to build. We did not see eye to eye and held different values in our lives. We had legal issues, we lost a handful of employees, and it hurt my culture.

Ultimately, I processed it all and analyzed the result - not as won or lost, not as failure or success - but in *cost versus value.*

The first thing I did was simply go back and look at all the little actions and outcomes that led to me being in this moment. I analyzed and realized all of the many mistakes I'd made along the way. I came to see that I had given more authority then I should have. Delegation is vital, however, there are aspects of running a company that require the owner's vision.

This was step one—I took the failure as an opportunity to see what I had done wrong so I could learn from it (and learn what I could do to never do it again). A lot of business and self-help books will teach you this step—because, yes, it is important. We learn largely through our mistakes. Then we learn how to do it better the next time. Each failure is the best opportunity for the most learning.

"Learn from your mistakes." You've heard that before, right? And it's true. To do it, we must review and understand "failure" on a deep level. That's how we grow, and *growth* has a high value attached to it.

However, we shouldn't just "learn from our mistakes." We should all also "appreciate our mistakes" so we may realize that these moments in our life are invaluable lessons that shape who we are, the lessons that begin to define our life course.

Even though I had selected the wrong executive team members and "lost," with my analysis through the cost versus value ratio, I had already learned that it was not a blowout loss. What showed me that this failure was, in fact, not even a loss but truly a victory, was what happened next—with *the things I would have missed* had things turned out differently.

What I really wanted to do was completely different from the old Lumegent business model. I wanted to mentor, teach, train, and consult. That was my love, creating the strategies that led other people to success—and there were a lot of things about the first incarnation of Lumegent that took me away from that. So, I wanted to go forward while removing everything else I never intended to be doing in the first place. MY SUCCESS in one area of my career had prevented me from building the thing I truly wanted.

With my choice to build MY SUCCESS, I got the company down to a bare-bones operation, and to further cut overhead (before we'd ever heard of anything called Covid-19), the new Lumegent went remote.

I knew this would fit my life. I felt like I could be more hands-on, more one-on-one than in that giant building we had previously been in. It clicked, and when the pandemic hit and a ton of businesses were buckling, we were already strong in our remote capabilities.

The business grew. We received opportunities with a Fortune 500 company in the hardware business. I consulted on a QR code campaign that brought business to their installation products during a time when this was falling. A concept to scan, get a quote, and remain contactless lifted numbers and brought in millions of dollars of revenue. People took note, and things really started to take off.

I signed on with an up-and-coming senior living company. Their team was strong, and we clicked well. I knew I was working alongside some of the best in the industry.

But the most surprising connection out of it all was with me and their CEO. As fate would have it, this company was run by that guy who used to scare the crap out of me back at Interlude, none other than kick-me-out-of-class Keith.

It was great to get to know him from a different perspective. After landing the account, I went up to meet him in his office. I took a seat in the executive chair and was surprised by the fact that it actually felt like my feet touched the ground. I knew I hadn't gotten any taller, it was just that in charting my own course, I felt a whole lot less pressure from outside forces. Even with guys as scary as Keith.

"I'm not sure if you remember me or not," I said to him after I introduced myself, "but when I started at Interlude, you scared the everliving daylights out of me." Keith laughed, and we moved forward positively. This person who I always felt was against me turned out to be a great and trusted colleague. A friend.

I think that's because everything runs in cycles. Life seems to continue to show me this, and the new Lumegent is a cycle, a rebirth of sorts. Not one built by some rulebook to a rigged game, but something along the line of what MY SUCCESS has always felt like. Lumegent is helping people the way I want to: old school and personal.

I worked to develop a culture with clients that make them feel like a part of my team, and myself part of theirs. With our connections, we all knew that we had each other's backs. That if it came down to it, we would fight in the trenches alongside each other. Everyone knew that everyone else cared, and they knew I was in it with them. It didn't matter if a client came to us with something we'd never done or that was completely outside our scope; we would help them solve their problems. It was unique, the client-vendor relationship I'd always dreamed of.

We continue to drive revenue and breed culture for all our clients, which we do by using only a portion of what they were spending with other "big league" agencies. We build connections with our clients, we build a team. It's a win-win all around.

I was sitting in my home office one afternoon, and I stopped and took it all in. I leaned back in my chair, thinking about how I'd stepped away from a multimillion dollar company and was now creating another one—and how this time just felt *different.* It felt different because I was doing work that I truly and fully loved; work that was not killing me but lifting me up. It felt different because I was home.

I was with Ren; at every volleyball practice and game, watching anime, shows and movies. I was home to teach her psychology and guide her. I was there.

I was with Sami; able to be there for her, guide her through high school. I didn't miss her graduation. I was able to walk her down the aisle when she married Brandon. I was there.

And I was there for my Jill. Our pizza and fries movie nights, dates, long conversations, and to have time with each other. I was there.

I was back with my family, doing the things I wanted, the things that built me up, that made me feel successful. I was able to be a husband and a father. I found MY SUCCESS.

If I can do it, anyone can. That's not a line. It's what I believe. And it's why I do what I do.

Don't believe me? Then let's connect!

Part Nine

"No amount of money ever bought a second of time."

- Tony Stark, Avengers: Endgame

IT'S ALL PERSONAL

Most business books I've read go through the background of a person's success but then fall short at the end. The reader is left asking, *Billy, how can I use this and apply it to my life?*

Don't worry, I'm not going to finish this book without providing some answers on how you can chart YOUR COURSE.

Let's dive into how *you* stop following the lie, how *you* stop playing the rigged game, so you can build YOUR SUCCESS.

First, I need to explain the balance. Without understanding that your personal life and business life are blended, we can't chart the correct course.

The old saying is "it's not personal, it's business." This is complete nonsense. It is either outdated or has never been true. We are not robots. I'm sure you've had a boss or two or faced a high-powered executive that made you feel we could be, but in the end, we are not.

We are emotionally driven people. Therefore, I focus on relationships because, in business, it is always personal. We are all working toward our own form of "success", each on a different path to what we find important in our lives. This means that every single person in the world of business has a personal agenda at work. Otherwise, why are they there if not for some reason to get closer to their own defined success?

It's all personal in the way we interact, make decisions, and work together. Sure, too much of anything is bad. Over time, the world of business started to push out personal feelings and issues determining that there was not a place for it in the world of business, but that is wrong. *This is a lie.*

Personal and business must coexist because we are human and we are not only at work, or only at home. It's a blended environment. Just like in your personal life, business exists. If you allow too much of it in then it can hurt your personal life in the same way. If you take too many work calls from home does it bother your spouse or loved ones? If you're "off work" but doing projects from home, doesn't this take away from your time to yourself or your family? But guess what? It crosses over. For most, you don't get to completely ignore your business when you go home, especially those running their own business, so why hide that our personal life comes to work with us sometimes as well?

But what we can do about it? It's a challenging balance to find the integration of personal and business. I find that the only real way to find balance is through the proper development of relationships. Building strong, positive bonds and surrounding yourself with people that respect your time will shape the path to your success.

It is more important to build a strong relationship with a client than it is to upsell the client or attempt to grow the revenue. I have years of proven success with this technique. It's simpler than it seems. Once the relationship is built, the upselling and growth occur naturally.

For the organizations I've created, it's a rare occurrence that I need to ask for a sale or attempt to push for more sales. Working with one of the largest organizations in death services, I started with a single project to restructure the marketing department; a task that would take only a few months with minimal revenue resulted in over ten million dollars in additional revenue from other projects.

How? By building trusting, long-lasting relationships. I never once asked for additional projects and opportunities, I simply built the relationships, showed the cost versus value in working with me, and allowed the client to ask me to take on each of these opportunities. I ensured they respected my time and I respected theirs.

Building relationships comes at a cost of time. Time, I'll continue to say, is easily the most valuable asset we have as humans. It is the one thing that can never be recouped once it's gone, and we have a very limited amount. I value time over all other values.

So, what is the number one thing I give my clients? My time. I spend time getting to know them at work and outside of work. I take a genuine interest in who they are as people just as much as the professional version of them. I get to know their families and I connect with them on a personal level. It can be as simple as going to dinner after a long day of work or spending my evenings at their family events while I'm in town. It can be taking them to their favorite concert and truly being part of the experience with them. It could be allowing them to openly vent and giving advice as a friend, not as colleagues or clients.

Sure I am spending my most valuable asset, but the relationship I am building will ultimately create respect and value for my time. I used my time upfront to build a lasting relationship with mutual respect for one another.

As the relationship is being built, if they need me, I am available. If they need support or made a mistake and need an out, I am there. I dedicate the same level of time and energy that I give to the personal relationships in my life, and that is what makes the difference. As the relationship forms, there is a deeper bond that grows between us and then the respect and value of my time is considered.

This differs from the standard vendor/client relationship. It becomes a partnership. This approach can be built with clients, co-workers, employers, and others. We become a team.

I build each professional relationship toward the goal of creating this team. A bond is formed when you are on the same team. Teammates work together for shared goals, respect is formed, and you pursue success together.

Think about the best relationships in your life, business or personal. Is there a mutual respect of each other's time?

Understanding that life is a blend of personal and business will allow you to approach your course differently. A course that guides you toward YOUR SUCCESS.

Regardless of work time or personal time, your time is valuable. As you develop relationships, you want to surround yourself with people that respect and value your time.

But wait a minute Billy, didn't you say that time is the most important asset, yet you explain how you give it away?

Yes. But this is where balance comes in. You need to find the balance that fits in your life to ensure you are taking care of yourself, your family and the time you give up is still aligned with your course.

Time is the most important asset we have, so we have to use it wisely in our personal life and in business life. This will support the development of relationships and work.

The key is to find the right balance of how much to give and who and where you give your time.

CHOOSING THE RIGHT JOB: If you are searching for a new job, ask the expectations of your time during and after work. Get an understanding for the expectations so you know what you are agreeing to. If the job requires you to always be on-call and available, how is this going to impact time at home? If the job requires you to work a graveyard shift, or four twelve-hour days, what will this do to your personal time? Time should be a prime consideration in cost versus value.

Before accepting a job, we typically ask about pay, benefits, and PTO. What about the expectations of the majority of the time? What about the time we spend during the week at work, and at home? Won't this be just as impactful as the pay?

At work you are trading your time for money, but that doesn't mean it should be all-consuming of your personal time as well.

Understand if the company you are applying to, or currently working at respects your personal time. Ensure your cost versus value (time versus pay) aligns with your goals. If not, I suggest searching for employment somewhere that will.

But Billy, what if I don't have a boss as I run my own company?

CHOOSING THE RIGHT CLIENTS: If you are running your own business, you can still control your time. Hours of operation (for those in the retail space) ensure you have days off. For those providing services or work with consistent clients, choose your clients wisely.

Although you work for yourself and you control your own time, many business owners struggle with self-respect of time. Entrepreneurs are taught that you say *"yes!"* to any and all business. This is part of the lie.

Then most entrepreneurs feel they must be involved in all aspects of the business. Learn to delegate!

You should still consider how taking on each client or project will affect your time as well as your own direct time being input to each new client or project. Using cost versus value, analyze if it is a good idea to take this client or project on, if you should hire support to reduce your time, or reject the client or project entirely.

For me, running my own business, I wanted to focus on the things that really mattered—doing the aspects of my work that I enjoyed and spending time with my family.

So, I decided to go down to a four-day work week. I'm testing it out now as I write this book.

This wasn't a instant shift. I didn't wake up on a Friday and declare, "Hence forth, I shall no longer work on Fridays!" It took planning and preparation. For the next month, I spent time rebuilding my calendar, discussing with clients, and planning longer workdays during the week to accommodate the extra day off.

This also means there are some clients I won't take on. Sure, I am missing out on the revenue, but I am gaining so much more of my personal time. *Cost versus value!*

I've hired the right clients—those that respect my time. As I approached them to move consistent Friday meetings, they were supportive. After a month, I've now begun to take Fridays off. It's still a work in progress, every so often I handle a few things on a Friday, but my course is heading in the right direction.

This approach also inspired Ren.

Noticing I wasn't heading into the office on Fridays lately, she asked about it.

"Can I do that too?"

I told her that if she wanted to, she would have to study longer during those four days on. She's homeschooled, so it's possible.

"But I'll get a three-day weekend?" she said, her face lighting up at the idea.

"If you work hard enough."

And so, Jill and I worked hard to get Ren's school week down to Monday through Thursday.

We did it because the ultimate currency there is and ever will be is Time. At 14 years old, Ren is already understanding this value.

We only get so much time, the body ticking away day after day. What matters is your life and how you get to spend your time. And coming from someone that has lost so much and almost died, time is the only value.

Study after study shows us that no one should be working beyond fifty-five hours a week. Consistently crossing or even nearing this threshold not only gives you a 30 percent increase for stroke or heart attack later in life, but it also ultimately limits your high-level production.

At points in my career, I was *doubling* that number, working hundred hour weeks for long stretches at a time. With all the stress and lack of sleep, the cost, as you read, was getting too high.

If you can find value in time, and find respect of your time, you're sure to find YOUR SUCCESS.

Part Ten

"He who has a why to live for can bear almost any how."

- Friedrich Nietzsche

CHARTING SUCCESS

For far too long, I went through life following what *others* would define as success, without stopping to think about what success was to me. This resulted in me spending every ounce of myself, to the point of death, to reach something I didn't actually want.

Let's prevent that for you.

Before you go too far in the wrong direction (or for those of you already lost in rough seas chasing the success of *others*), let's dive into correcting your course.

We'll start with one of my favorite words: *envisage.*

Envisage

verb

en·vis·age | \ *in-vi-zij* , *en-* \

envisaged; envisaging

1: to view or regard in a certain way

2: to have a mental picture of, especially in advance of realization

Words have power, and *envisage* is one of the most powerful for me. Maybe it can be for you, too. Practicing the concept allows us to get to places that we "see."

If we feel down in the dumps, for instance, we often lead ourselves to dark places. If we feel happy, we tend to end up in good places. To have a mental picture of something before it happens is how we manifest something. What we visualize has a way of getting us there; to envisage where we want to be in five years guides us to success.

It works out at sea, and it works with our careers and with our lives. And, to get on course, we all need to envisage what success looks like to us as individuals.

To find YOUR SUCCESS, you must first be able to develop a mental picture of what that success means to you and how it fits your life. To chart a course toward YOUR SUCCESS you must first identify if you are currently heading in the wrong direction.

Identifying the wrong direction is the first step in charting your course. There are key details that will follow you when you're not on the path of YOUR SUCCESS.

But Billy, how do I know if I am heading in the wrong direction?

If you are feeling lost, unsure, unmotivated, or lack joy when reaching an achievement, this is a sign you are on someone else's path to success and not your own. On this course - no matter how much money you are making or what your title is - you are also probably feeling overworked, underpaid, or your work feels meaningless.

Those on the wrong course also experience feeling depressed, angry, and out of control. We experience feelings of helplessness in our abilities to control our own life, and we feel like we are missing out on the things we want to do. For me, as you now know, it was always about missing out on spending time with the ones I love.

If you identify with any of the above sentiments, it is a sign that you are guiding yourself toward a version of success that doesn't fit your life—or who you are.

You may need a complete 180 in your course heading or maybe only a slight correction in your angle of movement. I work with people in all areas of course correction.

We don't need to flip your life upside down today, only to begin to steer your course in the right direction, toward the life you want. Like all journeys, this may take some time, but ensuring you are heading in the right direction guarantees that you reach the destination you intend to. And it starts with *envisage.*

See yourself in ultimate happiness. Get to know that place and that feeling. What you are doing and why. And how.

And then work backward—to get from where you are today to where you want to be.

So, let's envisage YOUR SUCCESS.

Below is a series of questions that will help guide you in your discovery process to identify what success means to YOU. Whether you are out in a sea of bad or currently on an island of good, these questions, answered honestly, will help you chart your path to YOUR SUCCESS:

Grab a pen and let's get started!

WHAT DOES SUCCESS MEAN TO YOU?

WHAT DOES SUCCESS MEAN TO YOUR FAMILY?

WHAT ARE YOUR REASONS FOR WORKING?

WHAT ARE THE TOP 5 IMPORTANT THINGS IN YOUR LIFE?

1.

2.

3.

4.

5.

DO YOUR REASONS FOR WORKING ALIGN WITH YOUR TOP 5?

WHAT EFFORT ARE YOU WILLING TO PUT IN FOR THOSE TOP 5 THINGS?

ARE YOU WANTING A BETTER BALANCE OF WORK/PERSONAL LIFE?

ARE YOU WANTING TO GAIN A LEVEL OF CONTROL OVER TIME?

WHAT ARE YOUR GOALS PERSONALLY?

____

____

____

____

____

____

WHAT ARE YOUR GOALS PROFESSIONALLY?

____

____

____

____

____

DO YOUR GOALS MEAN SACRIFICING TIME, ENERGY, ETC. FROM YOUR TOP 5?

____

____

____

WHAT ARE YOU WILLING TO SACRIFICE TO REACH THOSE GOALS?

____

____

____

____

____

____

____

ARE YOU WORKING TOWARD THE CAREER OR JOB YOU WANT?

ARE YOU WANTING SOMETHING TO CHANGE IN YOUR LIFE? WHAT IS IT?

DOES YOUR FAMILY AGREE WITH YOUR CHANGE?

WHAT THINGS CAN YOU DO TO WORK TOWARD THAT CHANGE NOW?

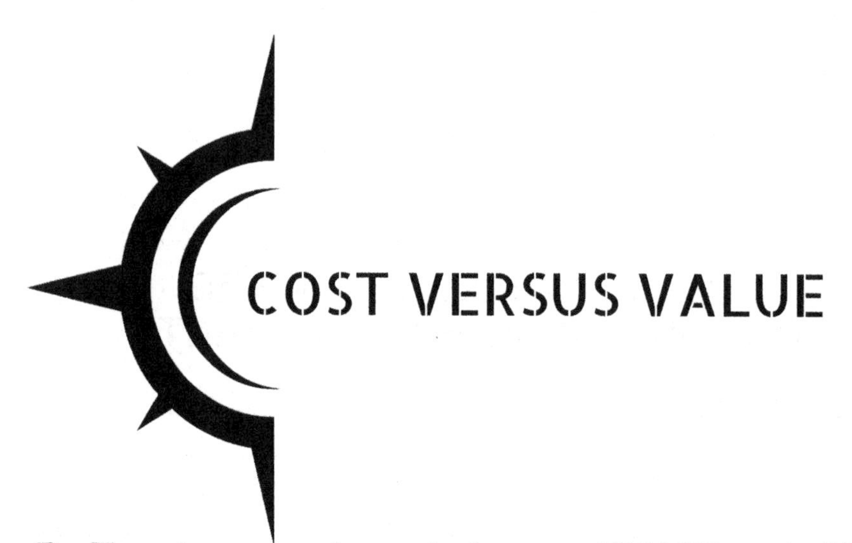

COST VERSUS VALUE

Now that you understand what your VALUES are in life, we need to be able to plug them into a formula to ensure the equation is right. I've already given a fair amount of time to cost versus value throughout the book, but before we chart your course, I want to be sure we have a solid grasp on the model. Let's dive in a little deeper.

In short, cost versus value can be applied to large decisions or everyday decisions. Simply take the thing you are considering, then compare it against what it takes to get it—the time, money, material items, energy, sacrifices, and whatever else contributes.

Let's take it down to a basic example: If I asked you the *cost* of a candy bar, you'd maybe say one dollar, but what is the *value* in comparison? Does your enjoyment of the candy bar exceed the expense of a dollar—yes or no?

Now, let's factor in that you are making ten dollars per hour. This small additional factor now compounds the equation.

We can compare even deeper by saying that based on your rate of pay, for six minutes of work, you can enjoy a candy bar.

Is that treat worth it now?

Now, let's say you make a hundred dollars per hour. The candy bar decision becomes a bit easier, doesn't it? You could purchase this candy bar by working a little over half a minute.

Another way to consider this is on a monthly basis. Let's say after paying your bills, you only have twenty dollars left at the end of each month. A budget this tight might make you reconsider the value of that candy bar. Sure, you could take that last twenty bucks and buy twenty candy bars—but would you?

But Billy, how can a candy bar make a difference in my life?

With a tight budget, entertainment, for example, is a high expense. Say a streaming service runs at seven dollars per month. For seven dollars, you can have access to endless amounts of content, movies, sports, and shows. A candy bar will bring a moment of satisfaction, whereas a streaming service could bring hours of entertainment per month.

If you stop a simple purchase of candy bars, those funds can be put toward something else. Candy may be more important to you than entertainment and vice versa, but that is for you to decide when you compare.

Now—an example that doesn't involve purchasing, but *time.*

If I was to offer you a job that pays two million dollars a year, you may immediately accept my offer without even taking the time to hear what the job is or what it may entail. Instant acceptance—the two million fills your ears and that's all that matters, right?

Not so fast.

Because next, I tell you that to get this job, you have to give up almost all of your personal time. You must travel constantly, you are rarely home, missing out on much of your family life. Then, I explain that the anxieties and pressures of the job may result in depression and health issues. Finally, I tell you that there is zero recognition or praise, but often you feel like you are going to lose your job regularly.

Still want that two million?

To sum up my soapbox of cost versus value: it is everywhere, in all walks of life. And I find taking it into account regularly has a way of simplifying our decision-making process to get us on a course that best fits *our* version of success.

Incorporating this simple yet effective concept into our daily lives is a good thing to do. Try charting out a day or a week of cost versus value to see if you are on the right track—or if you may benefit from some course corrections.

NAVIGATING TOWARD YOUR SUCCESS

Like cost versus value, many of the greatest things we can learn in life are not the complex ones but the simple ones. Treat others as you would like to be treated. Give to receive. I find that often the best learning is from knowing, from intimately understanding, simple concepts.

Let's keep it simple. I like to use the acronym—SEA.

SEA

Stop. Evaluate. Accomplish.

STOP: The first step is to stop, so we may reflect and plan. Too often, we just *keep working*. We keep on toiling. We put up with things that we shouldn't and never stop grinding. For a lot of us, we don't stop pushing too hard until something tragic happens—our health fades, a car crash wakes us up to something, or once-great relationships are now not so.

What I am encouraging you to do, right now, before the crash, is to *stop*. Pause and reflect on some of those answers you gave a couple of chapters back. Give some time to what is important to you, and what you want from life.

We all can and should make changes today, because tomorrow may already be too late.

So, stop—and then *reflect.* Think about the changes you want to make, today, and how they can begin to alter your course. Defining and understanding what you feel is successful will allow you to properly think through and assemble a plan toward YOUR SUCCESS. Using the questions above to define YOUR SUCCESS, you can properly think of the things you want more, or less of, in your life.

Once you've taken the time to stop and reflect, it is time to begin to *plan.* Sure, failures in life are going to happen, but without a plan, we are essentially setting ourselves up for that outcome.

You can't, for instance, just walk into work tomorrow and tell your boss, "Sorry, I no longer work on Fridays."

You can, however, make a plan. If a four-day work week is something you think may benefit your life, you can speak with your boss and see what is possible—and better yet, you will have *planned* for the meeting, with a clear outline of how you will stay on top of things if your objective is achieved.

Conversely, your plan may be to start looking for a different job, one that fits within the days/hours you seek. It all starts with a *plan,* which comes from the *reflection* you've done after you've *stopped.*

EVALUATE: Now that you've stopped, reflected, created a plan, and you are ready to determine if your cost outweighs your value, or, if you are getting good value on the costs you are putting into your navigational course.

Since we've touched heavily upon the concept, I will simply say, that for the evaluation portion of SEA, do it frequently. Evaluate and re-evaluate as you continue to fine-tune your plan. Endeavor to not do things blindly, but always with great intention. And, as always, if you find that your cost outweighs your value - no matter how big or small - have the confidence to diminish the ego so you can change it up.

If you need a cost versus value reminder, head back to page 212.

ACCOMPLISH: The old adage tells us that "our result is based on the effort we put in," and that the harder we work the greater the reward. That is largely true—but not 100 percent.

It is *how* we approach that work that is key. Those clients and friends of mine who I know are living their true success do so by working with their authentic self—doing things they love, with soul, with creativity, with all of themselves.

For me, there is nothing better to describe this type of success than the word **Meraki.** From the Greek language, this word has no true counterpart in English.

Meraki

verb

*me·ra·ki | \ may-rah-kee *

A Modern Greek word, derived from the Turkish "Merak" (Labor of love, to do something with pleasure), is applied to tasks, usually, creative or artistic tasks but can be applied to any task at all.

1. To do something with soul, creativity, or love.

2. To put "something of yourself" into what you're doing.

3. To do something with passion, with absolute devotion, with undivided attention.

In short, it's definition is along the lines of "something done with this soul and creativity and done with great passion and/or love."

But when it is used in Greece today, it often holds the connotation of someone putting themselves fully into whatever they are doing. The Japanese word, zen, means roughly the same thing: that we are at our best when our mind is clear, and completely given to what we are doing, even if it is painting a fence or washing a car (thanks, Mr. Miyagi).

On your course-charting journey to find your islands of good (and especially those weathering the seas of bad) please keep in mind **SEA**. Set sail with: *Stop, Evaluate, and Accomplish*, this will ensure the course you chart will guide you toward YOUR SUCCESS.

UNTIL NEXT TIME

Last Tuesday, Jill came to sit with me on the couch. She leaned over and looked at me.

"Do you feel successful?" she asked in that soft voice of hers.

I thought about Jill's question. I thought about that word… "success." I thought about my life: I'm not running a one hundred million dollar company anymore. Nor do I have over a hundred employees or locations around the world.

But am I traveling nonstop for work? Am I missing out on my family? Am I working myself into an early grave?

Nope.

I've built Lumegent into a company that fits MY SUCCESS, and I am proud of it. I am doing the work I've always wanted to do—the type of consulting, executive coaching, and life coaching that gets to change businesses and lives. And I work Monday through Thursday. Rarely over twenty-five hours a week. This means I get all the time I want with Jill, Ren, and Sami.

I thought about my wife's question. I told her that I felt more successful than I ever have in my whole life—but that I just wished I could help *more* people in *more* ways.

"So do it," she simply said.

I love that woman. She's always helping me believe. And here I am, wrapping up the book I never knew I always wanted to write.

You've witnessed some of my tragedies, seen some of my successes, and hopefully learned a bit about yourself along this journey.

You now know how I've been out at sea many times, lost in that sea of bad looking for islands of good. You've seen me find some open, teal waters only to struggle because I was seeking a version of success that wasn't my own.

I hope you've seen that we have a choice.

The premise that there is only one kind of success is a lie. There is a rigged game out there, and it is only when we choose a different course, based upon who we are rather than what is expected of us, that we can defy it, and that in defying it, we are ultimately defining ourselves. All you ever have to do is navigate toward your version of success. Whatever that looks and feels like, to YOU.

Because - and trust me on this - if I can do it, anyone can.

Acknowledgments

Thank you to all of you who have, in one way or another, found a way to impact me—my life, my career, and my family.

To my publisher, *Stephanie Pierucci*, my editors, *Jonathan Grant, Dale and Hannah Chaplin*, and my production/project manager *Julie Husch*. Thank you for helping me share my story with the world.

To those few whom I will always call "Boss": *Matt Leal, Jason Giovannoni, James Gann, Don and Misty Fike, Jamison Gosselin, and Bill Janess*. Thank you for teaching me discipline, focus, and kindness in leadership. You have all taught me more than you know.

To other colleagues who may not realize how significant your impact has been on me: *Ashley & Jeff Fetter, Peter Dibble, Brandon Eller, Kai Hsiao, Matt Keck, Mike Spates, Wendy Maldonado, Paul McGlynn, Greg Muzzillo, Todd Kelly, Sean Sweeney, Kathy Doherty, Steve Falk, Ijonas Kisselbach, Jason Smith*, and many others. Thank you for allowing me to connect with each of you.

To the teachers in my life that made an impact: *Mrs. Barnes, Mrs. Starr, Mrs. Goings, Ms. King, Mrs. Congrove, Mr. Rutledge, Mr. Perazzo, Coach Buchan, and Sherry Black*. Thank you for providing me with motivation and hope - for guiding me when others had given up.

To those there for me when I was growing up in all those seas of bad-*Oasis Castillo, Raymond Aguilar, Andrew Rico, James "JJ" Maragh, Kirk and Eric Dillard (and the entire Dillard family), and Raymond Lee.* Thank you all greatly.

To the people I met on the diamond. It's crazy to think that joining a softball team would amount to so many strong, deep, friendships-*Daniel Anderson, Brandon Bird, Jake Sommer, and Cary Jaques.* I am thankful to you and your families for always being there for me.

To the friends I don't see every day but always have my back when I need them- *Victor Morrow, Zack Pio, Alex Rice, Dan Stasik, Gary Monardo, and David Lewandowski.* Thank you all.

To "the crew." The people that always stay late. The people that I can always count on. The ones always there for Ren and Sami. Thank you, I love you all. To *Emily & Kevin "Doc" Tunsil.* Your family is our family. I can always count on your support and love and late night zombie runs. To *Grace "Rika" Eddy*, thank you for staying true to yourself, sticking with me, and always ready and willing to game! To *Andy Androwick.* Getting a nomad like yourself to stay close to my family means the world to me. To *Malia Seronio.* I am so proud to see you finally finding your island of good. Can't wait to see what you do next. To *Mikel Williams.* Damn, you've stuck it out with me. Who knew discovering we have the same birthday would turn into a brotherhood? 8/18! To *Kim and April Duong*, through humor, anime, and martial arts, you're always there for me. And to the "newbies", *Gabby Stone* and my BFF *Katelin O'Keefe.* Welcome to the crew!

To my second family. You took me in when I was lost out to sea. My second Mom and Dad, *Cheryl and Jay Caldwell*, thank you for being parents to me and grandparents to my girls. To *Grandmom and PopPop, CJ and his family, my loving Aunt Cynthia,* and my kid sister *Sydney.* This family means the world to me, I love you all.

To the entire *Janess and Powell families.* You've opened your homes, shared experiences, and offered me a place at the dinner table. I thank you, you all are appreciated and loved. Special shout-out to *Josie!*

To *Mike and Ginny Janess.* Thank you for allowing me to be part of your family, for trusting me with your daughter and granddaughter, for wanting the best for us, and for taking a chance on me. It's not always been easy, but it has always been with love and good intentions. I love you both.

To my sisters—*Tara, Tasha, and Tiffany.* We've faced a lot together, but know that I am proud of you, and I believe in each of you. I know you are all capable of finding YOUR path and YOUR SUCCESS.
I love you all endlessly.

To *Mike Anderson.* Although brief, your life was impactful. You gave me a best friend, showed me courage, and helped me find myself. Steve and I miss you, especially on April Fools.

To *Steve Snyder*, words cannot express what we've faced together. You defended my wife and me when the world turned on us. You protected me, never judged me, and have always been there for me. I love you and your family and am proud to call you, my brother. We broke our generational cycle like we always said we would! Thank you for always believing in me and for being my first call.

To *Kevin Dodson*. You are one of the most amazing people I have ever met. You've always had my back, and I will always have yours. You build me up and make me feel I can conquer the world. There is no crew without you, Luffy, and Zoro, to the grand line and beyond, together. Love you, brother.

To my *Father, Bill.* You may be gone, but your lessons live on through me. You were my best friend and the person that knew me best. I miss playing catch most of all, but I use your lessons and talks to improve myself and help others every single day. As you taught me, I will always Adapt, Overcome and Survive. I love and miss you.

To my *Mum, Dee Ann.* You have always loved me, had my back, and wanted a good life for me. I learned love from you. You taught me deep compassion that I will never lose regardless of who wrongs me. You are an amazing, strong, and beautiful woman. Even as life beat you down, you encouraged me and gave me all you possibly could. Thank you for always loving me. I love you greatly.

To *Samantha. My Sam-Sam,* Sami. The girl that surprised me. Having you as a daughter has been a joy. While I miss our movie marathons and late night dance parties, watching you mature into an incredible and independent adult gives me more pride than you can ever know. You prove it is possible to choose the life you want. And to your husband, *Brandon.* B, you are like a son to me, and I'm immensely proud of you. But I'm still a game up on you in MLB. You both remind me just how powerful young love can be. I love you both.

To *Keiren*. My amazing, beautiful, quirky, unique, and brilliant Ren. The day you came into the world, my focus changed. I take pride in everything you are and the things you pursue. I see so much in you, and you can truly do anything. Stay focused, stay determined, and you will find your course, YOUR SUCCESS. Remember, I always have your back, I am always on your side, I will always be here for you, I will always be here to help you solve your cases, or even just to listen. I love you. And as always, how many hats?

Then, to the one that made it all possible, the fearless girl, the love of my life, the one that stood in front of a broken, scared boy and told me with a single look in her eyes that I was worth something. The one person who always knew I was capable of more and saw through my generational cycle to SEE me. None of this would be possible without you, and I wouldn't be the person I am today without you, my love, my one, my only, my now, and my always. Thank you for being the person you are and always believing in me.
I love you, **My Jillian.**

There is so much more I'd like to say. So many more people I'd like to thank. But in short, I want to thank you all for joining me on this crazy journey of mine.

—Billy Thompson

CHARTING SUCCESS

FINDING YOUR WAY IN THE OPEN SEA

Too often, we just keep working. We put up with things that we shouldn't and don't stop grinding until something tragic happens—our heath fades, or a car crash wakes us up.
So, stop. Pause and reflect to what is important to you, and what you want from life. Then build a plan that guides your toward YOUR SUCESSS.

You are ready to compare if your cost outweighs your value. Endeavor to not do things blindly, but always with great intention. And, as always, if you find that your cost outweighs your value, no matter how big or small—have the confidence to diminish the ego so you can change it up.

The old adage tells us that 'our result is based on the effort we put in,' that the harder we work the greater the reward. That is largely true. But not 100% true. For, it is how we approach that work that is key. Work with your authentic self—doing things you love, with soul, with creativity, with Meraki.

On your course-charting career out in those seas of good and bad, keep a mind of SEA. Set sail with: Stop, Evaluate, and Accomplish.

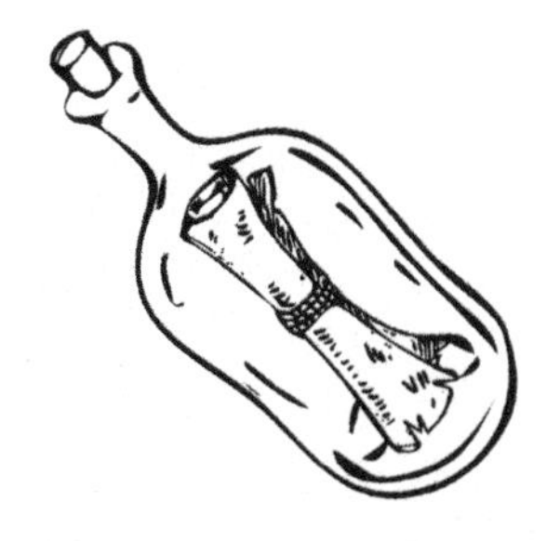

Get In Touch

Thank you for joining me on this journey and learning about finding SUCCESS. But please, don't stop here. This is just your first step in charting your course and I invite you to choose one or all of the following ways to connect with me, to keep creating your path, and to continue working toward reaching YOUR SUCCESS.

Learn more, connect, sign up for group and/or private consulting, schedule appearances, and more directly at: www.lumegent.com

Or You Can Follow Me at:
www.linkedin.com/in/billythompson-lumegent/
www.instagram.com/lumegent
www.facebook.com/lumegent

If you prefer email, send one over to:
chartingsuccess@lumegent.com

Or Scan the QR Code:

Made in the USA
Las Vegas, NV
14 July 2022